A Bowl of Perfect Light

A Bowl of Perfect Light

Stories of Forgiveness,
Reconciliation, and Repairing the World

MEGAN MCKENNA

ORBIS BOOKS
Maryknoll, New York 10545

Founded in 1970, Orbis Books endeavors to publish works that enlighten the mind, nourish the spirit, and challenge the conscience. The publishing arm of the Maryknoll Fathers and Brothers, Orbis seeks to explore the global dimensions of the Christian faith and mission, to invite dialogue with diverse cultures and religious traditions, and to serve the cause of reconciliation and peace. The books published reflect the views of their authors and do not represent the official position of the Maryknoll Society. To learn more about Maryknoll and Orbis Books, please visit our website at www.orbisbooks.com.

Published by Orbis Books, Box 302, Maryknoll, NY 10545-0302.

Chapter Four, "Coming Home" was adapted from Megan McKenna's "A Parable of New Beginnings," *St. Anthony Messenger* (November 2016).

Manufactured in the United States of America

Library of Congress Cataloging-in-Publication Data

Names: McKenna, Megan, author.
Title: A bowl of perfect light : stories of forgiveness, reconciliation, and repairing the world / Megan McKenna.
Description: Maryknoll, NY : Orbis Books, [2024] | Includes bibliographical references. | Summary: "Stories and teachings from various spiritual traditions to guide us in our call to forgive, reconcile, and repair our world"—Provided by publisher.
Identifiers: LCCN 2024009548 (print) | LCCN 2024009549 (ebook) | ISBN 9781626985896 (trade paperback) | ISBN 9798888660454 (epub)
Subjects: LCSH: Reconciliation—Religious aspects—Christianity. | Forgiveness—Religious aspects—Christianity. | Conflict management—Religious aspects—Christianity. | Interpersonal relations—Religious aspects—Christianity.
Classification: LCC BT738.27 .M37 2024 (print) | LCC BT738.27 (ebook) | DDC 234/.5—dc23/eng/20240328
LC record available at https://lccn.loc.gov/2024009548
LC ebook record available at https://lccn.loc.gov/2024009549

For all my relations,
Friends of God

Contents

Introduction

And suddenly you know: it's time to start something new and trust in the magic of beginnings.

—Meister Eckhart

I greet you from the other side of sorrow and despair, with a love so vast and shattered it will reach you everywhere.

—Leonard Cohen

Behold this day, for it is yours to make.

—Black Elk

These last few years have been fraught with violence, trauma, and injustice that impacts individuals, communities, the church and nations. Looking at our history, the litany of unexpected, devastating events, and what we and even the earth have had to endure, can be exhausting and overwhelming. We've seen climate disasters; COVID-19 impacts; and deaths, especially among the poor, the elderly, and others in jeopardy from inadequate health care. These years have been further impacted by loneliness, isolation, discouragement, despair, and grief. Wars are escalating across the globe, as are acts of terrorism and mass shootings. We are facing disrepair; shatterings; broken relationships; and torn communities in search of healing, restoration, resurrection.

In my work with communities, so many have been reeling from the recent discoveries of burial grounds in Canada and the US, as well as the generations of lost children torn from their families, transported to boarding schools rife with abuse, forced labor, destruction of cultures, languages, religious practices. The result of those abuses has been consequential: disappearances, suicides, alcoholism, drug addiction, lack of health care, breakups in family relationships, all piling up on top of each other.

The world has been forcibly turned upside down and our lives pulled inside out. Where will we find respite and repair? All of us face an unknown future sensing we are *in over our heads*. We are short on resources, connections, and the energy to cope, let alone deal with all that must be changed to re-form our lives, relationships, and institutions for a strong resurgence of life and shared joy.

We hope for Incarnation: for an ongoing Advent, God becoming flesh and dwelling among us, accompanying us as we seek to live *our lives ever more abundantly* and gracefully, uncovering God's presence in abiding justice, forgiveness, and peace that binds us together as the beloved children of our God.

As we stand facing an unknown, difficult, and even

fearful future, there are steps and practices for the journey that can help us. And there are stories that show us the way. Here's one from the book of Exodus. We read of the Israelites having left Egypt, the land of their enslavement, on their way to the Promised Land. They are on the road to freedom and liberation.

They have endured two centuries of exile and repression, but now they have a destination ahead of them, which is worth everything. They have been told through Moses, "When you take this nation out of Egypt, you will serve God at his mountain [Sinai]." But just seven days out from Egypt where they have known oppression, persecution, misery, slavery, the murder of male children, the kidnapping of the young girls, torture and forced labor, they meet an impasse. In front is a sea of water, with Pharaoh and his army racing after them to block their journey and return them to slavery. Here's where the story begins, at that impasse, seemingly trapped. An old Jewish midrash adds another story to the text of the Exodus story.

The people stand before the sea and hear the clamor of the army coming up behind them. They are trapped. What should they do? There is no escape. They must decide.

It is said that they break up into four groups, disagreeing strongly on what they should do. The first group decides in despair to throw themselves into the sea—better to die than to be butchered in a losing battle. The second group also despairs and encourages the others to give up and go back to Egypt and be enslaved once again. The third group vehemently decides to fight, to go to war against the vast Egyptian forces. And the fourth group says, "let's pray."

But Moses will not agree to any of the options. This is what Moses cries out to the people: "Fear not, stand by and see the salvation of God which He will show you today. For as you have seen Egypt this day, you shall not see them again, forever. God shall fight for you, and you shall be silent" (Exodus 14:13). Moses delivered God's message to all the groups. For those who wanted to throw themselves into the sea, he says, "Fear not." To those who would despair and go back, he says, "Stand by and see the salvation of God which He will show you today. For as you have seen Egypt this day, you shall not see them again." To those who would go to war, he tells them, "God shall fight for you." And to the last group that wants to pray, he declares, "You shall be silent."

God directs all the groups. God said to Moses, "Why do you cry out to Me? Speak to the children of Israel, that they should go forward" (Exodus 14:15). The Israelites are to journey to Sinai, to stand face to face with God there. So, no matter what stands as an obstacle to be confronted, all are to move forward. What threatens us can be overcome. The sea will be split and there will be a way forward toward freedom, toward liberation and wholeness.

In another midrash story related to this one, it is told that at that moment the people were told, "go forward," one or two daring souls did just that, diving into the water yelling to the others, "Come! We can do this!" And when those few entered the water, the water responded and pulled back, laying bare the ground hidden beneath the sea.

Each of us as individuals, and together as part of small groups, must be daring and bold—and dive in, moving forward to face each day and begin the process of becoming whole again, being healed, restored, and living with dignity and grace.

Living in the freedom of the beloved children of God, made in their image and likeness, reveals something of God in each of us: the need for us to become what we were born for, life with one another restored in justice and compassion, in love.

That is where this book begins. There are stages of the journey that require decisions, that are suffused with restorative practices. These are the only way we can live in relationship and in community, and the only way we can restore a devastated world. And the journey begins with forgiveness: being forgiven, asking for, giving, and sharing forgiveness with all. This is not a solitary action, but rather one that affects us in our communities, in our lands. Mutual forgiveness means that in reconciliation, we walk together again. Then together we learn to do justice, enacting that which restores dignity, integrity, and wholeness in all areas of our lives.

The other side of repair or restorative justice holds others accountable. We hold others bound (responsible) for their actions and seek to undo the harm that has been done. This is how the processes of repairing the world, repairing our souls, our relationships, and all our institutions begins.

Throughout these stages of repair, we are called to live in a justice that doesn't seek violence, we are called to mourn, to grieve, and yet balance our lives with hope, with joy, with delight and the shared experiences of setting one another free.

We learn communion, to live as one with others and to rise, lifting one another up to live with passion, knowing peace, sharing bits of glory, joy, compassion, and the wild moments of being truly alive, even in ecstasy with one another.

We believe and declare to each other that we are the children of God, the brothers and sisters of Jesus, family with one another, sharing the same Spirit. We have his words to proclaim to us "No matter what, go forward, I am with you. Fear not."

At the supper, Jesus shared with his disciples—with all of us—the night he was betrayed, he tells us how to live, he reminds us who we really are, and he invites us into who we are meant to become in him. Some of his last words are etched into our hearts, memories, and souls.

> As the Father has loved me, so I have loved you. Live on in my love. You will live in my love if you keep my commandments, even as I have kept my Father's commandments and live in his love. All this I tell you that my joy may be complete. This is my commandment: love one another as I have loved you. (John 18:9–12)

We are to live loving others, as Jesus, and our God Father loves each of us, all of us. We are to live revealing God's image—of one who loves, in service to one another, careful of one another, intent on making sure others have a chance to live, with love as their driving force. This is a commandment to live with joy, to share joy, and to expect to know joy—joy that is complete when shared with others. But there is more:

> There is no greater joy than this: to lay down one's life for one's friends. *You are my friends* if you do what I command you. I no longer speak of you as slaves, for a slave does not know what his master is about. Instead, I call you FRIENDS, since I have made known to you all that I heard from my Father. . . . the command I give you is this, that you love one another. (John 18:13–15, 17; emphasis mine)

We were created to be the friends of Jesus, the friends of God, friends with one another. This is our destiny, our meaning, our calling. This is what it means to believe in and follow Jesus, to be his disciples, to be his friends.

And so, we begin this journey of becoming, this way of being in the world guided by Jesus's own words and actions that we will repeat over and over again in all our relationships and in so many moments of our lives.

And the journey of becoming—of liberation—is the journey of forgiveness. As Jesus goes to the cross, tortured, in agony, he continues living with love, refusing to do evil, speaking the truth, doing justice, tending to all others with compassion, and relating to everyone with forgiveness and mercy. The Gospel of Luke tells about his crucifixion, a violent execution, as he is crucified with two other criminals. "When they came to the Skull Place, as it was called, they crucified him there and the criminals as well, one on his right side and the other on his left, Jesus said, 'Father, forgive them; they do not know what they are doing'" (Luke 23:33–34).

In his suffering, Jesus's first words from the cross are among his last words to his friends (and the world): *Father, forgive them.* Our lives of soul, spirit, heart as human beings made in God's image begin, speak, and fulfill these words over and over again. *Father, forgive them. Father, forgive us.*

With Jesus, we pray always: *Father, forgive them.* It is Jesus's foundational prayer with and for all of us, all ways. We are the Father's beloved children along with Jesus. The Father hears us, listens to us, and responds to us, the way he heard Jesus, listened to Jesus, and responded to him. And the Father responds in the power of the Spirit by raising Jesus from the dead! The outcome of forgiveness is resurrection, is new life, life for our bodies and souls, life in God's Spirit shared with Jesus, shared with all of us.

We are all God's relatives. All people are our relatives: our brothers, sisters, mothers, fathers, our children, our aunts and uncles, cousins, and, even more, our friends of God with Jesus. In the Native American communities where I gather with friends to talk about healing, to share stories, and to speak about repair, there is a saying both among the Lakota people and many other Native American and First Nations people that simply proclaims *all my relations.*

These words echo Jesus's own prayer that we all belong to him.

> I do not pray for them alone. I pray also for those who will believe in me through their word, that all may be one as you, Father, are in me, and I in you; I pray that they may be [one] in us. . . . that they may be one, as we are one—I living in them, you living in me—that their unity may be complete. (John 17:20–23a)

We are given for (forgiven) one another, with one another. With God we seek to be one in them, to be whole, to be holy, sacred in God's sight, all of us together.

Over twenty years ago, I experienced what these words mean and they have lodged in my soul, my memory, and my heart, rising up in other situations or when I wonder what will come next.

About four weeks after September 11, I returned from overseas to the US. I climbed a mesa west of Albuquerque and walked among tourists from all over the world; I stood in awe of the desert floor, the high stone mesas and traditional adobes jutting up into the sky, the vast horizon, and the late September sun. At the end of the tour, someone asked the Native peoples gathered to sell their fry bread and pottery how they had heard about 9/11, since only traditionalists live up on the mesa. There is no electricity or running water. Immediately, practically every Native person flipped out their cell phones and said "same way you did!" There was initial laughter. But then someone asked, "What did you think of what happened?"

There was a heavy silence for a long moment and then every Native person moved together closely and began to chant the phrase *all my relations, all my relations.*

There was stunned disbelief as one of the elders spoke for all of them and said, "We are so sorry, it was our fault. It never should have happened." As the tour group listened, no one moved and no one understood what he meant. Then an older woman continued, saying, "Those poor people! How they must have suffered to do such a thing as a last resort. How could we not have noticed and responded to them before they were reduced to such horror and violence against others?" And the chant began again, "*All my relations. We are so sorry, all my relations.*"

The tourists left, awkwardly and silently. I stayed and listened as the Pueblo people talked, reflecting on what happened that day. Later I heard other Native communities in measured response, respond similarly—we are all one and we must learn that, and begin to take responsibility for the horrors around the world—the ones that are the product of military choices, economic systems, and nationalistic power. Until we start here, bending, learning to be flexible and not to just react to all that happens in the world with violence, wars, terror, heightened security measures, imprisonment, and profiling, predicated on fear and hate of others, we can have no hope that there will never be another tenth or twentieth or other anniversary of anything like this again—anywhere in the world. It is time for hope, for forgiveness—that gives acknowledgment of what was done, and its causes, and a firm purpose that the circumstances that create this kind of violence will no longer be a reality in the world.

We must begin the process that will undo the harm that was done. We must forgo the rage, the hate, and the systematic violence of military and security measures. We must forbear that we live in a world of over eight billion people all struggling to survive with grace. And we must live with a measure of human dignity that does not take for granted all we have, and how we received it, even as others barely have a chance at life.

We must forgive—we must begin with the words of forgiveness as a mantra that can transform our minds and souls. When we forgive, we do not consider all others as possible enemies but as possible neighbors, allies, and friends. And then we must forget—in the sense that we must make new memories, start relationships anew, open doors of possibility with different ways of relating to one another as equals, both and all intent on the fullness and wholeness of life shared and lived together as one.

This book is a sharing of our forgiveness journey. It looks at how we accept the forgiveness God offers, how we ask for forgiveness, and how we return the favor to all others and then seek to live reconciling our differences and creating harmony. In this journey, we then learn how to live justly, with justice that is restorative, imaginative, and creative, building bridges and opening doors to others.

How do we undo the harm we have done, or have known in our own lives? How do we practice what is known as *tikkun olam*—the Jewish concept of repairing the world as a way of life: repairing our souls after violence, death, trauma, and near unbearable grief.

How do we then cultivate the art and work of repairing relationships, institutions, and systems that defile the human community?

After we together examine the experiences and moments we all know in our lives, hopefully we will come to a deeper understanding of what it means to live with dignity, liberated from fear and violence, in freedom as God's beloved children, sharing wholeness, being holy and aware of the sanctity of each other—all others.

This is when we taste resurrection life: the fullness of grace, being loved and capable of loving others back, as friends. Even loving those we perceive as our enemies, not yet made friends. And in doing so, we will know peace on our earth, among one another and all creation.

Yes, it is truly a daunting task; yet it is what we were born to be, living as "all my relations," all one in God who is the community we are invited to live and abide in, as God's beloved friends with all living beings that share earth, God's universe.

We will all learn to sing our part in the one song of glory that we have been given as a gift when creation was begun and was "in the beginning" that still continues and will evolve gracefully as the mystery of divine life in our place and time.

As you journey into forgiveness, community, repair, restoration, and toward resurrection, I trust this book will serve as encouragement with its stories, practical advice, shared wisdom, and hope along the way as we go forward, together.

REFLECTION

The words that follow—and the short quotations that begin and close each chapter—are hopes and suggestions (and sometimes challenges) that other friends of God have shared with me and their communities and the world as they speak, write, and pray. They are cherished and memorable lines that are like energy for our minds, hearts, and souls as we live and mature together, continuing our journeys home.

And for those who want to go deeper, connecting the thoughts and ideas of reconcilers, poets, singers, writers, prophets, and fellow companions in our struggle to be forgiving, liberated, and healing people helping one another to live in communion with one another, a combined bibliography–suggested readings list has been included at the end of the book.

To pray is to dream in league with God, to envision His holy visions.

—Rabbi Abraham Heschel

Praise the path on which we are led/Praise the roads on earth and water.

—Joy Harjo

The transformative power of love is the foundation for all meaningful social change.

—bell hooks

We do want to be beginning, but let us be convinced of the fact that we will never be anything else but beginners all our lives.

—Thomas Merton

May the Lord only preserve in me a burning love for the world and a great gentleness and may God help me persevere to the end in fullness of humanity.

—Pierre Teilhard de Chardin

If you can't fly, then run. If you can't run, then walk. If you can't walk, then crawl. But whatever you do, you have to keep moving forward.

—Martin Luther King Jr.

1

The Mystery of Forgiveness

Forgiveness liberates the soul.

—Nelson Mandela

To forgive is to set a person free and to discover that the person was you.

—Lewis Smedes

The secret of my identity is hidden in the love and mercy of God.

—Thomas Merton

Forgiveness. Forgiveness is the gospel message—the Good News of God to the human family. We are forgiven, made whole, made holy in Jesus's Incarnation, life, death, and resurrection. Forgiveness is not just a practice but a way of life. To forgive is to give life in God, to share in God's way of relating to people, to each other, as the beloved children of God.

Why begin at forgiveness? Forgiveness is a way of relating that relates to and develops into other ways of living with God and one another on earth. And this way of life, of following Jesus as a disciple, is a process—with steps or practices—that is both an individual experience and a communal one.

In this chapter we will look at forgiveness, being forgiven, and forgiving others. We begin here because this is the first step, followed by reconciliation, then restorative justice or restitution.

Restorative justice, the remaking of community into communion, evolves into at-one-ment. And it entails undoing the harm done to others and the harm we've experienced ourselves. This approach to the steps of forgiveness, the way of life in community and communion, is the call of what the Jewish community calls *tikkun olam*, the repairing of the world.

This multilayered repairing of souls, repairing of relationships, and repairing of systems is literally in Hebrew related to repairing damage, and restoring balance (to the extent that it is possible), and accepting and living with the consequences of one's actions. This involves taking responsibility in public for what we've done and to gracefully make amends.

In a traditional religious sense, this is the underlying basis for what is given as *penance*, after the confession of sins. It is meant to be an active righting of the wrong, not just prayers or sorrow. *Tikkun olam* is a lifelong process that enfolds forgiveness and reconciliation, and for those of the Christian faith, it is rooted in our baptism and in living resurrection life together now.

The second step of reconciliation is a mutual one. The word itself means *to walk together again*. This mutual forgiveness is part of life in community, a gift of the Good News of the gospel shared with us.

The life of forgiveness can be understood, lived, in the sign of the cross, which is the sign of forgiveness and reconciliation. We are signed with it, even made in this image. It's a gesture we also bless others with. This ritual images our relationship with God that is a vertical relationship. But it is only as deep and true as our relationship with others, that horizontal reach, extended out to all, even our enemies.

We begin with forgiveness because this process contains a hope of making all one, of bringing all together again, to remember again, in unity, in communion, of making peace, bending to the needs of the community, as all communities hope for and seek. To dwell in peace, the peace of Christ, the Risen Lord, is the beginning of living resurrection life now, initiated and begun in our baptism. And the *end* result of forgiveness and reconciliation is in keeping, extending, and deepening communion among everyone.

Forgiveness begins with justice and acknowledgment. What is due to the other? The acknowledgment of the reality that we are all sinners. *Sin* is a term many don't like to use and carries with it so much baggage, but it means to *miss the mark*.

In the steps of forgiveness, only after acknowledgment and only after justice is rendered for ways we have missed the mark, can we begin to speak about mercy. It is God who does justice. And mercy is born out of justice. Justice relates to what a person deserves. But mercy is not about deserving. No one ever deserves this depth of compassion and forgiveness moving us to be reborn in our hearts and lives.

So, let's begin here: with forgiveness and sin. And with a story that helps us look at ourselves and begins to look at what that missed mark is in our lives and hearts.

It's important to note here that the stories in this book that originate from Native communities were shared with me and repeated back by me to the storytellers until the story was remembered correctly and "the telling was right"—and I was given permission to share these stories, such as this one, originating in Native communities in the far northwestern part of the US, Alaska, and Canada. Its main character, the Raven, is notorious in Native stories. The raven is a bird that is found everywhere in the world, and Raven sees and hears everything. It loves to steal things, especially anything that shines or glitters and so Raven is also a trickster and a thief. And because the bird is found everywhere, Raven also is a symbol of the Great Spirit, God's presence that is all knowing and ever present.

Once upon a time Raven was out flying, but he was

hungry. Raven was always hungry and so he was also hunting and looking for something to eat. As he flew high above the land, over the wide-ranging forests, he noticed a clearing in the woods that he hadn't seen before. And upon further investigation he realized there was a small village, just a couple of houses. He landed in front of the largest dwelling. It was quiet and no one seemed to be around. He immediately realized it was a smoke house.

The smell was strong and inviting, and he knew that there would be many fish drying inside on the walls. He entered and looked around, amazed. Every available piece of space on the wall held drying racks, and they were packed with fish being smoked and drying out. He looked around. The house was empty. He checked out the fish and spotted the largest fish he could find with a first survey. He grabbed it in his beak and took it back to one of the tables, dropping the fish on it. He stood over it and with his open beak, dove into the flesh. But just at that moment, the fish moved! It flew off the table, through the air, and splat! The fish was back on the rack. Raven was stunned, looking around, but his fish was gone—back where he got it from.

But he was not to be deterred; he was hungry. He went back and looked over the racks. This time he decided to take a medium-sized fish and brought it over, dropping it on the table. He put one of his spindly legs on it to hold it down and went to bite into the ripe flesh again. BUT again, the fish flew off the table, upending him, flattening him on his back.

Looking around again, he looked more closely to see if there was anyone in the house, lurking in the shadows, where it was cool. But there was no one. He was growing more cautious now, but he was also hungrier. Once more he went and selected a fish—a small one this time and carried it back, laying it down carefully. Again, he tried to bite into the fleshly part of the fish and bam! It was gone again, back to its place on the rack.

Now Raven was both angry at not getting anything to eat, but he was a bit scared, too. What was happening? He realized there must be many spirits in this place that were guarding the fish, and they were much stronger than he was! He decided in an instant he'd better leave. It wasn't worth fighting whatever was taking the fish so he couldn't eat.

He ran outside, staggering in the bright sunlight and stood silent for a moment, getting his bearings. There was still no one around that he could see. But then he noticed something on the ground beside him. It was a dark shape, and as he hopped around, it followed him! He tried flying to a tree, then back toward the building, but it followed him no matter where he went. Now he was afraid. He rose and took flight, but the dark shape followed him, even as he flew higher and higher—it was there—on the ground below him.

Then he knew: it had accidentally discovered and entered the land of the shadows, and it would follow him forever now. Now, the shadows' spirits would know him wherever he was and know his tricks and that he was quick to steal and be a thief, taking what did not belong to him.

And so, they say, now you know how you got your shadow that follows you everywhere, looming over you at times, shifting and disappearing to a thin line, but always there. Your shadow, your companion that knows, keeping you company and reminding you that no matter what you do, you are not alone, you are known, and you are seen, even if you steal, take what is not yours, or intrude and are not aware that others do see you. Like Raven, we are never alone.

This insightful story is called Raven's Shadow and it is probing us, evoking memories, and alerting us to our behaviors and attitudes at any time. We can think of the shadow as ominous, eliciting some sense of fear or foreboding, of being watched, but the shadow can also remind us of what we call our conscience, that which questions us on our actions and intentions. The shadow can even be the Great Spirit, the Spirit of God that hovers over all creation, ever present accompanying us throughout our lives.

In ancient times, in the early church, it was said that the Spirit was the Shadow of Jesus bent over the lives of his followers, with them always, echoing Jesus's words from the last line of Matthew's Gospel that promised "behold I am with you always, even to the end of time."

That presence of the Spirit is important to hold on to as we fail, we sin, and we all miss the mark of what it means for us to live as believers, as followers and disciples of Jesus. And we can't talk about forgiveness, repair, or justice without talking about sin. In scripture these are always related.

Scripture sets up an understanding about sin. And baptism promises to deal with sin. Everyone deals with missing the mark. And they may not like the work, but trauma has to do with sin, injustice, violence, and dishonesty.

Sin is communal and structural. And the Spirit proves the world wrong about evil and injustice. Sin marks the Christian, and the pledge we make at baptism is all about forgiveness, justice, restoration, and honesty in dealing with our personal and communal sin.

For the first three centuries of the church, understanding sin and its harms was essential, as sin (and thus repair and forgiveness) related to

- how you relate to God;
- how you relate to others;
- how you relate to your community, to the larger structures of church, and regional/country governance.

When we understand sin as relational and connected to so many others, we see we are all in need of forgiveness—much like shooting a basketball, aiming, and missing the shot.

In the early church, there were two types of sins that individuals confessed after baptism. The first was not telling the truth, especially related to authentic faith, if someone claimed to be a believer, a member of the church. To make that claim falsely, was called apostasy. Your word was your life and your truth, and God is the Spirit of Truth. Within this category was stealing, a form of dishonesty.

The second sin was to do violence or harm to anyone for any reason. What that meant was that if you were a soldier, you were not allowed to be baptized. Even in the military. If you could kill or harm anyone obeying another's orders, then you were not practicing Jesus's words: "love one another as I have loved you." And when you left the military and entered the church, the first penance you were given was working to give or save life to make up for the harm.

There were also sins individuals confessed when, after baptism, they were in relationship with others. The first was unfaithfulness. In marriage, this was a betrayal of marriage vows, adultery, or the disrespect for one's wife or husband. For those living as single, widowed, or unmarried persons committed to single-heartedness toward God and the community, missing the mark looked like a heart not focused on God or on the good of one's community.

Lack of forgiveness was another sin. Forgiveness was meant to be given for all things, requiring a mutual forgiveness that led to reconciliation and then atonement/restitution and restoration. In the early church, this required a process and time. If you refused to forgive another person (after three times being requested to do so), then you yourself would be refused forgiveness. In the church, in our communities, we are bound to one another. If we accept God's forgiveness for ourselves, but refuse it to others, we have missed the mark of giving as graciously as God has given it to us.

In the early church there were many "Christians" who committed what was often called the unforgivable sin. This happened during times of persecution, when people denied their faith, or worse, in order to protect themselves, named others who would then be questioned and persecuted. Rather than forgiving apostates immediately, the church would tell them to speak to a person who had refused to deny their faith. Sometimes that meant visiting them in prison, as they waited to die, and praying with them for forgiveness as they died. The person who had sacrificed to the point of death, someone willing to die for the truth, would in this circumstance forgive the one who denied knowing Christ or who betrayed others.

And last, there were two sins individuals confessed in relation to the community of church. The first sin was refusing to share, holding greed and selfishness in regard to resources, food, clothing, shelter, money, and all excess. The early church set as imperative, as the book of Acts reads, giving to the poor and "to give to each according to their needs." The other sin was not being a servant in the community, not putting one's gifts and skills at the service of the community, and not using the gifts of the Spirit given at baptism and confirmation for the life and growth of the others.

This list of sins related to the church can sometimes feel

exactly like a list of dos and don'ts. Each of these relates to how we live in relationship with ourselves, our neighbors, our communities of faith, and God. The words might look daunting–sin, apostasy, hoarding. But they are the details of something that is rooted in how we understand relationship, faith, and community.

Missing the mark relates directly to how we are living in relationship with others. And by asking the following questions, we can understand what these questions ask of us, what we might need to confess about how we missed the mark in our relationship to others, to ourselves, to our communities, and to God.

1. Is it harder for you to forgive someone or to ask forgiveness from another person you've harmed?
2. When someone harms you, when relational trust is broken, what sin is hardest for you to forgive? Why?
3. Have you ever needed to ask forgiveness from a group you belong to, or as a member of a group, did you need to seek forgiveness from another person in the group?

Beginning with these questions helps us develop the tools for the first steps of forgiveness. Another way to understand what we might need to confess as missing the mark is through the insights gleaned from the gospels and the early church communities where the marks of living in whole relationship were spelled out. These include the following:

1. Do no harm or violence to anyone.
2. Speak the truth.
3. Forgive all, for everything, all the time.
4. Do justice, and practice restorative justice (corporal works of mercy).
5. Share. Give to the poor, according to their need.
6. Endeavor to love faithfully, in all your relationships.
7. Serve the community, especially those most in need, victims of violence, the poor, widows, orphans, aliens, strangers, immigrants, outsiders.
8. Love one another as God has loved you.
9. Bear your share of the burden of the gospel.
10. Bear one another's burdens.

Living wholly in community, in relationship with others calls us to also live in the light of our baptismal promises:

1. As children of God, live now in that freedom.
2. Resist all evil. And for the sake of others, offer the alternative of hope.
3. Live under no sign of power but the sign of the Cross, as the Trinity and your faith community seek to reveal God together.

It begins with forgiveness. A gift we are given. A gift we give others. We are always offered this gift. Forgiveness is essential to life, intimately connected to how we live, impacting our bodies, minds, hearts, and souls.

Forgiveness is an ordinary experience most of the time—and in some circumstances and relationships can also be extraordinary.

As we consider what it means to miss the mark, to confess, to forgive—and the call to live in wholeness in community—there's a story about a young couple in the church that might be helpful to consider. In this story, the young couple asks a question of another couple in the church: "How can God forgive sinners? Isn't God mindful of all the hate and meanness that people do and are capable of?"

In response, the other couple asked them, "Aren't you the third generation of a master carpenter that makes fine furniture? If you have a hand carved table or cabinet that got scratched or dented, would you throw it away?" They answered, certainly not. "True it has a scratch but the rest of the piece is still intact." The couple who owned one of the rocking chairs that others had carved and kept as a treasure in the family said, "You share the same spirit of God the creator who looks at us, and sees all the nicks, dents, and flaws, even gouges in the wood, and still considers us precious and worth all the work that went into its creation." Then they laughed and added, "In fact, it gets better with age! We wouldn't trade it for a new one any day!"

That's how forgiveness works. Nicks, dents, and flaws and the beauty of the original continues to shine.

In another story, this one, a parable from Luke's Gospel, often called The Pharisee and the Publican or the Tax

Collector, we are given a perspective on sin and forgiveness worth taking to heart. In this story, Jesus shows us the missed mark, the genuine, and how faith, how prayer, moves in relationship.

> [Jesus] then addressed this parable to those who were convinced of their own righteousness, and despised everyone else. Two people went up to the temple area to pray: one was a Pharisee and the other was a tax collector. The Pharisee took up his position and spoke this prayer to himself, O God, I thank you that I am not like the rest of humanity—greedy, dishonest, adulterous—or even like this tax collector. I fast twice a week, and I pay tithes on my whole income." But the tax collector stood off at a distance and would not even raise his eyes to heaven but beat his breast and prayed, "O God, be merciful to me a sinner." I tell you, the latter went home justified, not the former; for everyone who exalts himself will be humbled, and the one who humbles himself will be exalted. (Luke 18:9–14)

The "religious" person "spoke this prayer to himself" while the tax collector actually prayed to God. The Pharisee's opinion of himself is warped in his own favor, as is his criteria of what is good and what might be sin. Sin, missing the mark, doesn't seem to factor much at all into his assessment of himself.

And while the tax collector doesn't confess any particular sin, he acknowledges who he is before God: one who is lacking in faithfulness and obedience to God's opinion of what it means to be a human being who fails and who is in need of conversion. He knows he's missed the mark; he knows he is in relationship to God and others. The Pharisee sees himself as not in relationship, as someone "above" others, "as not like everyone else." Where one man throws himself on the mercy of God, the first one gives an accounting of himself as someone in no need of God, in no need of God's forgiveness or mercy.

The one is self-righteous and self-satisfied, even contemptuous of others, ignoring any of his own shortcomings, and so, he can't even see the goodness in others. He may be observant in observable practices, even law-abiding on specific issues, but inwardly lacks integrity and is incapable of true prayer: of standing before God and being seen for who he is from God's vantage point.

The other is focused on God, in humility knows his own life might be in shambles, but knows he wants to be otherwise, more what God hopes for him to become.

Forgiveness is about admitting that "yes, we are like the others" and not above others, and not so special in who we are because of our station in life.

When we pray, do we come out way ahead of others in our own estimation (thinking we are better religiously, politically, economically, culturally, or because of ethnicity or color) like this "prayer" of the Pharisee? Or do we come out, understanding our position of need, accepting God's grace and forgiveness.

Jesus probably told this parable about these two men at a time when people went to the temple to pray at the afternoon sacrifice, which focused on atonement. The one prays out loud, standing out, advertising his piety and self-worth, announcing that he is "religious," setting himself apart from the other and separating himself from the covenant of God with his people. The words he speaks are not the words of atonement, the foundation of the prayer to God for the community: *Lord have mercy.* In the words of the story, we hear Jesus state that we stand with everyone else, we need to take responsibility for our actions and their effects on others, with others. One man considers himself holy but is haughty. The other man admits he's a sinner, but he is seeking God's presence and salvation.

Forgiveness—the gift of God always offered to us—is a gift to be also offered by us to others. In First Nations tribes and in Native American communities of the Carolinas region, they tell a story that reminds us how we are to accept forgiveness and how we are to share it with others.

It was early in the time after creation and a man and woman lived with each other, wanting to stay together. Most of the time it went well, but there were moments when they were at odds. The man didn't like the way the woman cooked, or she talked too much. The woman didn't like the way he took all she did for granted, and how he expected her to do all the cooking, cleaning, and preparation of the game he caught.

As winter finally came to a close, the man went out to hunt, and the woman stepped outside, reveling in the sunshine and fresh air. She wandered around, picking wildflowers and herbs she had learned were for cooking and for healing. The day was gone before she realized.

The man came home, having caught nothing, and he was angry when there was no food prepared. There was yelling and even pushing one another around. The woman finally left, running away, with the basket of flowers she held. She was fast and furious at him. For a few moments he sat down and fumed. Then he realized how harsh he was and remembered how she had done so much to keep them fed and clothed through the hard times. And he cried, realizing how he had hurt her. He got up and ran out after her. But she was fast and she had a head start on him.

She ran and ran, gasping for breath, and noticed tiny flowers. She slowed down and noticed small berries under the leaves. She stopped and began picking them, tasting them, tart blue ones. Then she remembered her anger and got up and ran again. But again, she slowed down when she noticed more new plants. She bent down, pulling aside leaves and found more berries, tentatively eating some. They were larger, black and juicy, and she sucked on them delighted. But then she heard him coming after her and got up and ran again, hard and fast. He was getting closer. But again, there were more plants and smells.

She thought, the Creator has left us many new things over the long snows and dark. Again, she sat down and picked more berries. These were sweet, some a bit tart, deep red, and unlike anything she had ever tasted. She rolled them around in her mouth, laughing at their taste.

Then he caught up with her, sitting in the patch of berries, her fingers and mouth red, smiling up at him. He crouched down beside her, trying to catch his breath so that he could say he was sorry to her. They say the Creator gave her a nudge, and she took a plump red berry and pushed it into his open mouth. He smiled. And he took one and fed it to her. They sat there and fed one another the fresh berries still cold from the night before.

After they were full, they got up and walked back home arm in arm. They were called strawberries. And whenever they fought or argued, they would go and get one or two and feed them to one another, forgetting their anger and making up.

It became the tradition that early in the spring when they would be ripe and ready for picking, the whole tribe would go strawberry hunting and bring back baskets of them. Then on a certain afternoon, each person would take a basket with them, and go visiting their neighbors. When they knocked or called out to them, and the door was opened, before anyone could speak, their visitor would place a ripe strawberry in their mouth, smile or laugh and leave, going onto the next house. It was their way of saying "sorry," let's forget all our angers and live again grateful for all the Creator gives us. The strawberries mend and heal our hearts when shared with one another.

> *My humanity is bound up in yours, for we can only be human together.*
>
> –Desmond Tutu

> *Where you stumble, there your treasure lies.*
>
> –Joseph Campbell

INTENTION, REFLECTION, RESPONSE

Rabbi Meir once said, "When a person enters the world his hands are clenched as though to say, 'The whole world is mine, I shall inherit it'; but when he takes leave of it, his hands are spread open as though to say, 'I have taken nothing from the world' " (Ecclesiastes Rabbah on Ecclesiastes 5:14). Maybe the opposite of forgiveness or what keeps us from giving or receiving forgiveness is "holding on."

Ask yourself:

- What do you hold onto that doesn't help you, but weighs you down, or even harms you?
- What is it that other people do that you hold onto—refuse to forgive—instead of letting it go?

Practice

Sit with your fists clenched. Sense how your body feels and how tightly your fists are clutching. Then slowly open your hands, feeling the release of tension and consciously let go of what needs to go.

2

I Forgive You

As I walked out the door towards the gate that would lead to my freedom, I knew if I didn't leave my bitterness and hatred behind, I'd still be in prison. If I did not forgive I would still be in prison.

—Nelson Mandela

The function of freedom is to free someone else.

—Toni Morrison

Forgiveness. How do we move, now, from understanding about forgiveness—why we need forgiveness—to what it means to forgive. How do I forgive another person? How am I supposed to forgive someone who has wronged me? How often do I have to forgive? Do we forgive everyone, all the time? Does saying the words "I forgive you" make it a reality?

And what about ourselves? Is it possible to forgive ourselves? And is that also another critical necessity?

These are perennial questions for all of us. And they are questions we must ask ourselves or others at different times in our lives.

Perhaps beginning with a story will help us see how forgiveness permeates our lives. It is an old story from Hawai'i. And a version of it can be found in *Tales from the Night Rainbow* by Pali Jae Lee and Koko Willis.

Once upon a time—each of our lives begins this way, entering time and space as a singular person. We are each born and when we are born, each of us is given a gift: a bowl of perfect light! We are to tend this light in this bowl with care and diligence all our lives. If we do, then there is practically nothing that we cannot do!

Think of it: swim with the fish, even sharks and orcas; fly with the winged ones; roam the expanse of earth, discovering water to drink, food, plants that are edible and useful for healing. We can grow in understanding and knowledge and communicate with others in language, even sing, dance, make music, and work with others.

But we can also neglect our bowl of light and worse—we can do things that destroy, mar, and bend things out of shape, misuse all sorts of things, even other people. We can act with greed, stealing, taking what belongs to another, breaking things in rage, and destroying what is good—even venting our rage and anger on others.

When we do this, we drop pebbles, rocks, and stones into our bowls; and some of the light wanes and is blotted out. Stones and light cannot exist in our bowl together.

The light struggles and moves, but the stones are inert and just gather in the bowl, blocking the light.

What do we do when our bowl becomes heavy and the light grows dim? It's easy really! All we must do is turn our bowl upside down and the stones will fall out. And the light grows stronger.

But it's hard to turn our bowls over alone, by ourselves. Each of us has a bowl of light, and we are gifts to one another. A most marvelous gift is a friend, someone else who helps us turn over our bowl, freeing our light, turning our life upside down.

Sometimes we must ask for help, and sometimes another comes to our rescue and does it for us, without our asking (this can take us by surprise, and sometimes we don't much appreciate it at the moment). But with time and others we can learn to watch what we put in our bowls of light. We can lay aside what is wrathful and violent, and we can nurture all that grows and heals on earth, even the silent music of the stars.

Remember stones and light cannot dwell together in your bowl. Seek light. What's in your bowl now?

In a sense this story speaks of sin—those heavy stones—that burden us and dim our light as well as the forgiveness that sets us free.

It's important to remember that forgiving and being forgiven is a process. There are steps in this process that help us to set others free. In doing so, we find we ourselves discovering freedom too.

To turn our bowls over and let the stones fall out, there

are five steps in the process of forgiveness that we can take, strengthening our light.

The first step is to FORGO those stones of bitterness, blame, vengeance, getting even. This means we refrain from reacting to, and attacking, others. This step entails stopping for a moment to reflect on what has happened, how we feel, and what effects the blame or unforgiveness has on us. We instinctively react when we experience hurt or have been wronged by another's actions or words. Often our *gut* reaction is an anger response, which is the other side of hurt. While we must feel what is triggered in us, this step requires that we seek not to react by immediately throwing it back at the other.

We feel the pain deeply, find ourselves crying, breathing hard, walking away, muttering to ourselves, holding onto something, reaching out to be with someone who will listen, comfort, and understand. But when we feel, we also must draw back and collect ourselves, making sure we do not escalate and provoke reactions. When we draw back and collect ourselves, this helps us seek to reflect on our reaction and with that pause, respond from a different place.

The second step is to FORBEAR. Most of us aren't used to doing this—ever. The scriptures tell us to forbear, to bear our share of the burden of the gospel, to bear our cross, the burden that is laid upon us by others. When we slow down, we can put whatever happened and what we are feeling into a larger perspective of our lives and the context of what's going on around us, and in other peoples' lives.

All of us do awful things: things that are mean, petty, thoughtless, insensitive to others, just as we are the object of others' harsh words or wrongdoing that affects us. We don't have to react or even respond to everything. Some things can just be left alone, put aside, and we can go on. But that is not to deny our feelings. Taking some quiet time allows us to see what has happened to us and in us and how it is connected to others.

The next step is to FORSAKE. That means we let go, stop clutching, holding tight to what has happened to us or how we feel and what we think we'd like to do in reaction to our pain. When we hold onto the pain and anger, we can beat the memory *to death*, picking at the scabs of the wounds we perceive others have inflicted on our psyches and hearts. We all know how to *feed the fire*, stoking it to a roaring pitch. But to forsake feeding the fire means we let it burn out. We put the past behind us in order to live in the present moment. Forsaking pushes us to turn aside, to turn our focus and concentration on something else, to put our energies elsewhere in places and people, in moments that are not connected to what has hurt us.

And then next up, we FORGET. This takes creativity and imagination as we seek to create new memories and experiences. Forgetting doesn't erase what happened between us or to us, but in a sense, we color over it and remake our relationships. We do simple, ordinary things: sending a note or an email card; getting together for a cup of tea or coffee, even a beer; and spending some time to establish some new parameters to our time with others; taking a walk; working out; engaging in a game; watching a movie; listening to music; visiting a museum, art show, even the zoo; playing with a pet together; making new moments that push whatever transpired into the background. All this takes time but moves us toward forgiving someone.

And the last step that can happen at any point, even repeatedly is to FORGIVE—using the word. To forgive, it helps to start with prayer, short and to the point, asking for the grace to forgive the other, especially aware of God's always forgiving us—over and over again. It also helps to look at them in a kindly light, remembering good things that might have been a part of the past, or even coming up with a litany of gratitude for them, seeing them in a new way. And praying the Our Father can set us up to find the place and time to simply say, "I forgive you, let's start again." "I'm sorry this happened this way." "Can we let go and go on?"

The next steps are to maintain the *usual* things that happen often in daily conversations and where we work, study, play, even worship. They are steps within a way of life, forgiving and moving on, opening the door to continue together.

But for more serious issues of sin within a community, the scriptures provide us with a different process of forgiveness for two people, where serious issues of sin need to be dealt with and faced differently, and with integrity.

In the Gospel of Matthew, chapter 18, we see that forgiveness is the glue that holds the community together as well as the various relationships within the community. Jesus's teaching reads:

> If your brother sins against you, go and tell him his fault between you and him alone. If he listens to you, you have won over your brother. If he does not listen, take one or two others along with you, so that every fact may be established on the testimony of two or three witnesses. If he refuses to listen to them, tell the church. If he refuses to listen to the church, then treat him as you would a Gentile or a tax collector. (Matthew 18:15–18)

Jesus lays the process out carefully. First, no matter the issue or problem, resolution focuses on the one to one. We are to go to the person we feel has wronged us and attempt to settle our differences together. The aim, the result of this meeting, is always to listen and to come together again with a sense of forgiveness and having made peace with one another. But in instances where the situation is not resolved, then the process brings in and includes one or two others. And, of course, these one or two others are not people chosen who are *on your side*, but rather people nonaligned with either person who can be honest and unbiased. The process mentions the testimony of witnesses, which means we are dealing with serious issues with consequences for the two involved and also others of the community.

Next, then, if issues aren't resolved in the smaller group,

going to the faith community, the church, to resolve the situation, to make peace, is required.

But in some versions of that text there is also another step mentioned: to go to the elders of the community, those who have been long associated with the group and have had a part in teaching, counseling, and forgiving one another. These are people with experience, background, and some level of wisdom, counsel, and understanding who can listen to both parties and bring a fresh take, and larger perspective, to the problem or the sin and the harm it is causing.

Last, the scriptures say, go to the church. Make it public and lay it out formally before the entire community, which will then be a part of the decision-making and decide the necessary response to the situation, and perhaps in that process a person or people will emerge who understand the depth of the problem that has developed and can offer guidance and insight.

In this process, which is carefully laid out, every opportunity is given; every chance to confront and deal with the situation with honesty and integrity is provided.

If step after step is followed and still there is no forgiveness, no reconciliation, the last resort is to "treat the other party as you would a Gentile or a tax collector." This saying has often been misconstrued, with communities responding with almost violent and destructive actions. In some instances, the community shuns the one who was judged to be wrong, or the people refuse to have any communication with that person. Worse, some groups reiterate the harm over and over, or worse still, the person is punished by being excluded from anything in church: meetings, worship, or Eucharist.

But all these punitive actions contradict everything in Jesus's teaching. When we ask, how Jesus treats Gentiles and tax collectors, we know he goes out to them, refusing to treat them as outcasts or outsiders. A Jewish rabbi discussing the call to respond to the one who offends with his congregation, said, the true response is to "love him more, love her more." Go out of your way to treat them with kindness and regard. Do not embarrass them in any way. Seek to draw them back into the community with acceptance.

This response is not one condoning the wrongdoing, but rather one that seeks to treat the one who has offended us with charity and a sense that the person is welcome, no matter what has transpired.

Jesus's words on how we are to treat one another continues:

> Amen, I say to you, whatever you bind on earth shall be bound in heaven, and whatever you loose on earth shall be loosed in heaven. Again, [amen], I say to you, if two of you agree on earth about anything for which they are to pray, it shall be granted to them by my heavenly Father. For where two or three are gathered together in my name, there am I in the midst of you. (Matthew 18:18–10)

In all situations and in all circumstances, singularly and as communities and the church, we are to forgive. We are to seek to hold accountable those who need to be held bound, and to set free, loose anyone who is open to being forgiven and who repents and turns toward the truth, in God and one another.

Jesus taught that the crux of all our prayers is to hold one another in community together, to draw people back in and to grow together in mutual respect and obedience to God's Word. Jesus is in our midst always, but when we are gathered in his name, and asking for what he desires, we experience something even greater: wholeness and unity in our communities.

As Jesus shared this teaching with his disciples, Peter, who had been listening to his words, spoke. He has questions on how this is supposed to be lived out. Hear his all too familiar question in the passage:

> Then Peter approaching him, asked: "Lord, if my brother sins against me, how often must I forgive him? As many as seven times?" Jesus answered: "I say to you, not seven times, but seventy-seven times." (Matthew 18:21–22)

Some translations read "seventy times seven," extending the number of times forgiveness is to be extended. In a sense though, Jesus is saying stop counting and start forgiving. It is never-ending and beyond any number. One translation of that passage in the Eastern tradition suggests that that means "always without limit," as Gerhard Lohfink explains in his book, *The Our Father: A New Reading*. The act of forgiving is meant to become as frequent and as natural as our breathing, an intimate part of how we live all our lives.

Many of us pray the words of Jesus daily, with the Our Father. Midway through the prayer we say, "Forgive us our debts as we forgive those who are in debt to us." More often the translation reads: "Forgive us our trespasses as we forgive those who trespass against us." But the word used refers to debt, revealing more than an act that infringes on or is committed against another. In fact, there are two ways to understand *debt*, here. The first time it is used, when we speak of our own debt before God, the word describes an enormous amount that is impossible to calculate, and impossible to repay. It is equivalent to paying off our country's national debt! The second time the word is used, *debt* stands for a pittance. Think of the way we talk about *nickels and dimes* in contemporary economics—suggesting that the seemingly small details of money are a usual occurrence and that debt must be dealt with consistently throughout life's daily experiences (Matthew 6:12).

In the version of this prayer in the Gospel of Luke, it reads, "And forgive us our sins, for we ourselves forgive everyone indebted to us" (Luke 11:4). We glibly pray this at every Eucharist and often in our personal prayers. Yet, it calls on us without any glibness. All of us know intimately how hard it is to forgive someone who has deeply offended and hurt us. It's excruciatingly hard to just say the words silently to ourselves let alone say them to someone else. It sticks in our craw, and we resist mightily. It is difficult to let go of the past and be present now to the other person and to all that it triggered in us. In *Life Thoughts Gathered from the Extemporaneous Discourses of Henry Ward Beecher* by Edna Dean Proctor, Henry Ward Beecher describes the reluctance and refusal to forgive:

> "I can forgive, but I cannot forget" is only another way of saying, "*I will not forgive.*" A forgiveness ought to be like a cancelled note, torn in two and burned up so, that it never can be [shown] against the [person]."

It is hard for us to let go of bitterness that seems to rise up in our throats over time like bile—even after we have said the words of forgiveness to ourselves, and to others. We struggle to forgive the same person over and over again. Our broken hearts crack again and again.

I recall my mother saying (and I expect many other people's mothers would say), "To err is human, to forgive is divine." But forgiveness is God's greatest gift to all of us, setting us free to live as the beloved children of God. Forgiveness, more than any other act, perhaps, makes us like God.

There is a story a rabbi told on the feast of Yom Kippur—the Day of Atonement for the Jewish community. It is a day to reflect upon our past, not just the past year, but our entire lives, repenting our failures and asking for God's forgiveness. Rachel Naomi Remen tells a similar story in her *My Grandfather's Blessings*, but when I heard it in the synagogue, it moved from words on a page, utterly tender and moving.

The rabbi came down from the *bimah* (the podium) where he usually preached. He went down into the congregation and read from the Torah. He went over to his wife and took his baby daughter out of her arms and walked back to the front of the synagogue. He held her up, showing her to everyone, and she was smiling broadly, squirming a little. Then she turned and faced him, her tiny hands reaching for his beard, pulling at it, giggling at him. He smiled back and then began a formal presentation on the seriousness of this day and the need for repentance, calling upon God to turn his face away from our sins and not hold anything against us this year.

The little girl wiggled and tweaked his nose. Her attention was diverted, and then she reached for the locks of his hair and found his tie. It was great for chewing on, though it didn't taste all that good, and she reached for him, snuggling with her arms around his neck, stopping his sermon. There was a moment of quiet while people watched the child and the rabbi with delight, forgetting anything he had said. Then he turned her around once again to face all of them and said something like "Look at her! Isn't she darling? Is there anything she could do that you wouldn't forgive her for?" Everyone was looking at one another and their own children, and remembering moments just like this one. Just then, she grabbed his glasses, putting them in her mouth and chewing on the end of one piece. There was laughter all around. And the rabbi said, "And when does that stop? When do we stop forgiving? When does it get hard and we begin with excuses and decisions not to forgive and stubbornly refuse to stay open to someone else? When did you stop? Do you remember who it was, or when or how old you were, or they were? When did you forget that you are a beloved child of God? And when did you forget everyone, absolutely everyone, is the beloved child of God?

We hear the underlying question, "How often has God forgiven us?" Do we forgive one another as often, and as many times as God has forgiven us? Forgiveness is hard work, but there are many times and places to make a start.

A Jewish parable tells of a king who fought with his son. And the son left in a rage. In retaliation, the king exiled him from the kingdom. Years passed with no communication. Then the king's heart softened, and he sent messengers to find his son and invite him to come back. But his son sent a message back to his father, the king, saying no, he couldn't, he wouldn't return. He had been so hurt, his heart still ached, and he was angry and bitter whenever he thought of what his father had done to him.

So, then the king sent a message to his son. It read simply: "Return as far as you can, and I will come the rest of the way to you. And we will meet."

This is the way we begin the process of forgiving someone else. When God forgives us, he doesn't come part way, he comes all the way, right up to embrace us and bring us back so that we can dwell together.

We have been called to heal wounds, to unite what has fallen apart, to bring home those who have lost their way

–Francis of Assisi

Holding a grudge doesn't make you strong, it makes you bitter. Forgiving doesn't make you weak, it sets you free.

–Snoopy

Ring the bells that still can ring. Forget your perfect offering. There is a crack in everything. That's how the light gets in.

–Leonard Cohen

INTENTION, REFLECTION, RESPONSE

- What excuses do you resort to when it is hard to forgive someone? Make a list of the usual ones that come to mind.
- Do you carry grudges now? Are there people you have refused to forgive? If so, make a short list of their initials and take a few moments to bring each of them before God and ask for the strength to try and forgive them.

- Are there things you need to ask forgiveness for? Are there people who need to know that you are sorry and that you need them to forgive you? Start in your heart if not with them in reality.

Rabbi Israel Baal Shem Tov once met a preacher who was forever berating his listeners for their sins. He would describe their evil deeds and what was in their hearts, telling them they would be punished for everything they ever did. The rabbi came to him and said, "Tell me, how do you know so much about sin, considering that you have never tasted sin yourself?" The preacher responded saying, "How do you know that I haven't sinned?" "Oh, said the rabbi, "I'm sure you would have used your own sins as examples, before you recounted all the sins of others so that they would know you speak truthfully, from your own experience."

The Taoist teacher Chang Tao-ling taught that it was good to write the name of the offended person on three pieces of paper. One was to be put on a mountain top for heaven. One was to be buried in the earth, and one was to be thrown into the sea. "Sin reaches to the heavens. Sin is to be buried. And from the waters of contrition, new life will come," wrote Yves Raguin, S.J., in *Taoism and Taoist Religion*. This also works well for those who have offended you, to put the past behind you and start living in the present for fullness of life.

Practice

Find or select a bowl of your own *perfect* or endless light and keep it in a place of honor. Daily or nightly, as you look at it, try to remember or consider those pebbles or stones you may have thrown into your bowl, inadvertently or deliberately, that may have caused others harm. Reflect on your stones and what you might do now to remove them.

3

Please, Forgive Me

You cannot conceive, nor can I, of the appalling strangeness of the mercy of God.

—Graham Greene

I wondered if that was how forgiveness budded; not with the fanfare of epiphany, but with pain gathering its things, packing up, and slipping away unannounced in the middle of the night.

—Khaled Hosseini

Forgiveness is hard for most everyone. Some find it's harder to forgive someone else. Others discover it's harder to ask for forgiveness. As we saw in the first chapter, in the early church, forgiveness was a part of living in community together, and understood in relationship. The early church traditionally held three ways to be forgiven: prayer, fasting, and almsgiving. There was once a joke that reflected this process: that all the early Christians must have been noticeably thin and poor, revealing two of these practices even in their bodies. These common Christian practices were a part of daily life. And the Eucharist was the rite for all seeking forgiveness of sins.

While we'll look at the Eucharist as the way of forgiveness in the following chapters, in this chapter we'll look at what it means to ask for forgiveness. In the early church, there was the matter of sin: what needed to be confessed, the content of the harm done; and what needed to be admitted to as what is (and is not) true in our lives.

Traditionally there were two kinds of sin: mortal and venial. Mortal sin was deadly, destroying the connection between God and us, and destroying the sinner's connection from all others. Venial sins were not considered deadly, more like minor infractions, revealing common faults and failures often committed in daily life.

Left between the two categories, though, was a huge gap. More recently in the church, that gap has been considered to be a third category: serious sin. These are infractions and actions that are evil and destructive, often repeated several times, leading up to the more deadly act that might be described as mortal.

Most of us can put a given *sin* into one of these categories quickly, almost instinctively. We know what needs to be confessed and know the behaviors to alter.

Understanding how we miss the mark, and this concept of sin, or what is considered evil, is not something found only in the Christian tradition, but rather is practiced throughout all cultures and religions.

In the Sufi tradition there is a story of Islam, in a version told by Rabia Terri Harris, that reveals this reality and how missing the mark develops and affects others, extending its tentacles of harm out into the community, beginning with one action by one person—much the way in Christian tradition, we see that sin operates relationally, harming community.

In the eighth century CE, Harun al-Rashid, the caliph of the Abbasid Empire, was a renowned figure of authority and vast power. Harun had once met with Charlemagne, and after their visit, Charlemagne sent him a gift of a precious rose bush that Charlemagne had tended in his own garden. When the caliph received the gift, he entrusted it to his master gardener, exhorting him to care for it and to bring him the first bloom when it appeared.

The gardener tended the bush carefully, daily, even nightly, checking to see its progress and growth, noting anything that might hinder its coming to bloom. Eventually the first bud appeared, and it developed into the most perfect rose the gardener had ever seen: lush, deep colored, and magnificent.

It was time to cut the stem and bring it to the caliph, but as he took his shears in hand, a nightingale started darting around the bush. The nightingale, it is believed, sings in ecstasy around roses. And the bird swooped down, flying straight into the one rose bloom. In seconds, its petals were scattered everywhere on the ground. The rose was destroyed.

The gardener was shocked, and fearful, but had to go and report to the caliph what had happened, and that there was no rose. He begged for forgiveness, saying that he hadn't known the nightingale was in the garden. The caliph was gracious and told the poor man that there was nothing to worry about. He would not be punished. He told him—what has happened, has happened. I do not blame you. But, he added, "keep an eye out for that nightingale. I'm sure more will come of this."

Relieved, the gardener returned to his work, weeding, fertilizing, and tending to the plants and kept an eye out for the nightingale. And sure enough, just days later, while hoeing around a bush, he spied the bird, now dead in the grass, killed and half-eaten by a snake. Amazed, he returned to the caliph to report what had happened. The caliph sighed and told the gardener, "This is the way of the world. Watch that snake—something will come of his killing the bird." Again, the gardener went back to his work. One afternoon he suddenly became aware that the snake was coiled, at his feet, wrapping itself around his leg. In a panic he hit the snake again and again, cutting it in pieces. He was relieved once again and informed the caliph that he'd killed the snake. Again, the caliph just said, "Watch out. You will one day have to deal with what you did to the snake."

Time passed, and the gardener got involved with others in the caliph's domain. He was caught and arrested for a serious offense. No one remembers what his crime was exactly: maybe stealing or perhaps he was involved in a conspiracy. The gardener was brought before the caliph and was sentenced to be executed.

Of course, the man pleaded for his life. He addressed the caliph using his own words. "Remember, my master, what you told me about the nightingale, then the snake, and now I find myself in the same position. Now, you will deal with me. But, master, when you have executed me, what will become of *you*?"

Hearing those words, the caliph was stunned. Now he had to decide what to do. Should he kill the man and deal with the consequences that he himself might face or release him and perhaps change the future?

The caliph relented. He pardoned the gardener who had taught him wisdom. Perhaps he also learned some compassion, under duress, being put in the same situation the gardener once occupied. Harun al-Rashid, it is said, responded, proclaiming, "Real strength and nobility is to choose forgiveness when it is in your power to exact revenge."

Opening the door to the reality of forgiveness, through this story we understand that forgiveness does as much for the one giving it as the one who receives the gift. Forgiveness not only makes relationships whole, it also works in our self-interest. This is how Archbishop Desmond Tutu of South Africa spoke of the effect forgiveness has on the one who forgives.

> When I talk of forgiveness I mean the belief that you can come out the other side a better person. A better person than the one being consumed by anger and hatred. Remaining in that state locks you in a state of victimhood, making you almost dependent on the perpetrator. If you can find it within yourself to forgive, then you are no longer chained to the perpetrator. You can move on, and you can even help the perpetrator to become a better person too. (From his foreword to *The Forgiveness Project* by Marina Cantacuzino)

Several of Jesus's parables teach us about forgiveness. The best known, and maybe the most beloved, is a collection of three interconnected stories: the Lost Sheep, the Lost Coin, and the Lost Son (perhaps better titled the Lost Child).

To understand the way parables work, it's important to know that this form of storytelling often starts with a usual beginning, as some very odd details develop culminating in an ending that throws you for a loop. An ending you never saw coming!

In fact, parables really don't have endings—they are stories thrown into your lap when you least expect it—leaving it up to you, to us, to finish telling—finish living—the story. That means there are as many endings as there are interpretations of the parable. It all depends on who you think the story is most focused on. Different meanings relate to different characters, and often minor ones surprise us by revealing wisdom and truth related to all the relationships in the story.

For instance, in the parable of the Prodigal Son (or the Prodigal Father, as it is usually titled), it is either the younger brother or the father who is singled out as the main character–interpretations all valid and insightful. Rarely, though, is the character of the older brother, or the community, or the relationship of the brothers included in the core meanings of the story, leaving untouched some of the deeper meanings of the parable.

All the usual interpretations are valid to one degree or another, but only seeing meaning on one level also distorts how a parable functions and operates as a story. Parables, especially Jesus's stories, are not primarily about one individual's relationship with God: parables are about the kingdom, the reign of God, and how that kin-dom creates a community that we often call the Body of Christ, a family of God belonging to the Father in the power of the Spirit, with Jesus as brother to us all, as brothers and sisters.

Parables are about making family, making a home and being the heart of a community of believers who call themselves Christians, followers, and friends of Jesus.

So, now, when we look at these three stories again, within the context of community making and family, we are open to seeing new relationships, and new understandings unfold.

When we first hear or read a parable, understanding the context of where, how, and why the stories are told is important to their meanings. Here's how the trio of stories begins:

> The tax collectors and sinners were all drawing near to listen to [Jesus], but the Pharisees and scribes began to complain, saying, "This man welcomes sinners and eats with them." So to them he addressed this parable. (Luke 15:1–3)

Context is crucial. Tax collectors, public sinners, riff-raff, the scum of the earth are all drawn to Jesus, listening to him, taking heart from his words. But in Jewish society, who you eat with is a theological and religious statement as well as a social and political one. The scribes and Pharisees are appalled by those who surround Jesus, by those Jesus is breaking bread with. He is breaking all the rules.

The Pharisees are scandalized that he welcomes these people and worse, eats with them at table. The leaders are resentful of the company Jesus keeps. And so, the three linked parable stories are addressed to them: to the ones who will not eat with "them," and so will not eat with Jesus. Here is the first of the stories Jesus tells:

> What man among you having a hundred sheep and losing one of them would not leave the ninety-nine in the desert and go after the lost one until he finds it? And when he does find it, he sets it on his shoulders with great joy, and, upon his arrival home, he calls together his friends and neighbors and says to

> them, "Rejoice with me because I have found my lost sheep." I tell you in just the same way there will be more joy in heaven over one sinner who repents than over ninety-nine righteous people who have no need of repentance. (Luke 15:4–7)

The story is short—just a few lines—but it sets up a bizarre situation and its effects, demanding that we engage in the proposition, questioning what we would do in any number of instances.

The plot is simple. A shepherd has one hundred sheep and one wanders off. But the first proposition is who among you wouldn't leave the ninety-nine and go in search of the one that strayed off? If you know anything about sheep, they are hard to keep together, easy to spook and stampede, and even an unfamiliar noise can set them off running in every direction. Practically everyone at the time of Jesus with their knowledge of sheep and herding would immediately respond, "No way, you don't go after one, leaving the others to fend for themselves. You might lose a lot more than just the one!" That's the first odd bit.

And then once the shepherd finds the lost one—often a fairly easy task as sheep tend to just plop down when they're tired or hungry and bleat, announcing their location. He lifts it up, puts it on his shoulders and lugs it home. A grown sheep might weigh between 70 and 120 or more pounds—so it's not any little lamb that he carries back.

Once home, he joyfully calls his friends and neighbors

to announce he's found this one errant sheep after leaving the ninety-nine out in the fields as a celebration gathers around this one returned to the flock.

He calls it *my* lost sheep. He is deeply attached to this one, it seems even more than all the others.

Then Jesus theologizes on the moment. This is the way it will be in heaven! Over one who repents rather than over the ninety-nine righteous people who have no need of repentance.

Until this point there has been no mention of *repentance* or forgiveness, when the offending *sheep* has been sought out and carried back to the group.

It's a very basic definition of *repent*: to turn around, to come back to the original place with no internal attitudes of harm to the group, or words or acknowledgment of why they left, or how they feel about being brought back. Rather unceremonious.

But here is one sheep—one turned around—and there is more joy than for any of the ninety-nine who are placidly (hopefully) still out in the fields munching away on their own.

The last line of the story is sometimes put this way: there is more joy over the one who repents (returns to the community) than over the ninety-nine *self-righteous* who seem to have no need of repentance. Notice how that really shifts the ending to the ninety-nine rather than the lone lost one.

This ending puts the Pharisees, puts us, too, squarely in the ninety-nine group who care less than nothing about the one that the shepherd went after. No one asks, "How do we feel about that one?" Or, even, "Why did it go off?" "Was it just hungry, disoriented, or was it driven off by others, and no one cared whether or not it left?"

What's going on with all the other sheep that they do not even notice the one that left? And how do we feel about the shepherd just up and leaving all those who remain to fend on our own? And do we experience that kind of joy about the sheep—about those who repent and return—welcoming them back with support and affirmation? The questions of the story both linger and implicate all of us.

Then a second short story follows, this time about a woman, in the parable of the Lost Coin. Again, Jesus tells a linked, short but evocative story.

> Or what woman having ten coins and losing one would not light a lamp and sweep the house, searching carefully until she finds it? And when she does find it, she calls together her friends and neighbors and says to them "Rejoice with me because I have found the coin that I lost." In just the same way, I tell you, there will be rejoicing among the angels of God over one sinner who repents. (Luke 15:8–10)

Those listening would have known where the ten coins were originally. It was the custom for a married woman to string her dowry, the ten coins, on a sturdy cord that she wore around her waist. This was her lifeline in case of the death of her husband, all she had to live on as a widow.

Every woman would have kept it on her person and guarded it closely. Losing one, she begins the search. She even lights a lamp to search in corners where it could have rolled under something or wedged into reeds or bricks, etc. on the floor. But losing one also means that the cord or belt that held all the other coins has broken and now she's in danger of losing even more coins. So, when she finds the lost one, the belt needs to be resewn and mended for the future.

Like the previous story, when the coin is found, she shares her joy with everyone around her, perhaps even using the lost and found coin to pay for a celebration, providing food and drink for her friends and neighbors to share her delight in averting a near disaster.

Again, the closing line: more rejoicing over the one lost, diligently searched for, and found, than the ones who are *safe* and sound still strung on her belt. This image more than in the first one reminds us that our being is closely bound to others, all on the same belt, so to speak.

The loss of the one endangers all of us, whether we know it or not. We are bluntly reminded that the loss of anyone—and a coin—affects us all. Implicit in this story is our need to search our own hearts and lives to see where we stand and if we are in danger of sliding off the string that binds us all together in community.

In the third and final story, at turns called the Lost Son, Prodigal Son, or the Prodigal Father, we hear a story that begins simply, like the others. A man had two sons. Recall the context of this story: scribes and Pharisees as one set of brothers and the tax collectors and public sinners (both men and women) as the other brother. This poor man has two fairly rotten sons. You can decide which son is worse than the other. We usually side with the one we believe, to us, is obviously bad. Or he isn't as bad as the other, we think, as we read the parable with an attitude of the judgment we hold.

In reality, the father treats both sons in the same manner, not only the one who returns home (for dubious reasons we might label as repentance—but the story doesn't record repentance, only a calculated selfishness driven by hunger).

Day after day, the father goes out waiting for his younger offspring. And the townspeople would have thought that dedication far overdone. But then when the older sibling won't come into the public feasting, shaming his father, he goes out again to meet the older son, leaving the party, begging and coaxing him back into the community and the family. Both sons are sought out and forgiven.

This is Jesus's Good News: we are already forgiven. It's up to us to accept it. And in accepting it, we in turn are asked to forgive one another and live in relationship to them with renewed openness.

In this parable we hear of Jesus seeking not only to forgive but to reconcile us to one another—in the context of the larger gospel story. This is the story seeking to reconcile the scribes and Pharisees and the other *good, not-so-good-bad people* with *them*—the ones that the Pharisees (and we) designate as the real sinners among us.

In all three stories Jesus is intent on reconciling us to one another in our families, our communities, churches, and even further, reconciling with those we consider enemies and even nations.

In these parables we meet the second phase in forgiveness—reconciliation: walking together again with each other in mutual forgiveness and with God.

Focusing on the father's relation to either one of his recalcitrant sons short circuits the parable of its intent to draw both the brothers back together. Only when both return, as good sons (and daughters) of their loving, long-suffering parent whom they are bound to by blood and now, hopefully love, is the reconciliation met.

This, and all three stories, end at the table where the tales were told—with the whole community, hopefully, coming together.

As Jesus ends the story, we are left wondering if any of the scribes or Pharisees or other onlookers listening to his words and reluctant to be associated with *them*, finally do draw up a chair and join them in the feast—with Jesus.

How do we seek forgiveness? How does reconciliation begin? These parables leave us lingering in the story—and our place in it. How does the story end? Who's still missing at the table, because of us? Who are we refusing to eat with?

If we do not eat with *them*, with one another, then we are not reconciled in our relationships and community, and are not welcome to eat at the table with Jesus either.

The Good News of God to us, who are the poor, the unreconciled, in this set of parables, in particular, is about all of us learning to cry out "Welcome home!"

You, me, we are all welcome at the table of the Lord. We've been found! Who are we bringing into the celebratory feast today?

Weeds too are flowers, once you get to know them.
–A. A. Milne's Eeyore

Let no one mourn that he has fallen again and again: forgiveness has risen from the grave.
–John Chrysostom

INTENTION, REFLECTION, RESPONSE

In the two parables: the Lost Sheep and the Lost Coin, questions that linger between the lines of the stories are, "What's it like to be among the ninety-nine left in the pasture? What's it like to be one of the coins still loosely attached to the belt the woman wears?"

- Notice that all of these stories end in joy! God rejoicing over both the lost one and those who are called to welcome the newfound errant one. Do you rejoice over others who return to the community (not "just" after a communal penance service but over those returning to the community of faith after being gone for a while)?

- Put yourself in the role of the shepherd going out after the lost one or the woman searching for the lost coin. What's it like? What do you experience? We are most accustomed to being the lost one rather than the one who goes and plays the role of the seeker who is intent on finding what is lost. Experience that intention of seeking out the estranged, finding them, meeting them, awaiting them with love.

When a Persian rug is in the process of being woven, it is hung on a large frame. Behind the rug, young boys and girls sit on stools and work on the back of the rug. The master weaver stands in front and shouts directions to the young ones on the other side of the frame. If one of the helpers makes a mistake and puts the wrong-colored thread in the wrong place, the master weaver lets it be and does not remove it or correct the error. Instead, he weaves the errant thread into a new design or changes the existing design to include the *mistake*.

When a finished rug is examined for its quality, weavers, sellers, and experienced buyers look for at least one, if not more, of these mistakes as marks of genius in a superb rug, according to Father Bruno Hagspiel, who relayed this to me.

Most of us spend most of our lives in the group of ninety-nine sheep or with the rest of the coins on the cord the woman wears around her waist. We live making mistakes and judging the *ones* who leave or are lost. But forgiveness and grace call us to be in community and allow us, along with the master, to weave it all into the tapestry of our lives, correcting and undoing the mistakes and failures by redeeming and converting them into beauty.

Reflect on some of your mistakes and weaknesses that God, with help from others, has redeemed and is in the process of redeeming during your life as you are woven into the rug of your community of faith.

4

Coming Home

God is a father to the fatherless, a mother to the motherless. God is my sister, my brother, my leader, my guide, my teacher, my comforter, my friend. God's my all in all, my everything.

—Thea Bowman, FSPA

As we saw in the previous chapter, Jesus is a storyteller, a master storyteller, whose favorite way of telling stories is through parables. And unlike stories from Western traditions that have a beginning, a middle, and an end with their *happily ever after* formats that we've come to expect, parables involve us in the stories in an entirely different way.

Recall how the parable story begins with a setup (often coming from a context or question giving rise to a particular story in response). Then the parable continues with odd bits and strange hints throughout. And finally, just when we expect it to end—it doesn't! It just leaves us hanging there—waiting, hoping, wondering—and curiously involved in the story itself.

Among storytellers, there's an apt description for how the parable works and what it intends to do to us. *The story begins when the teller stops talking*. This saying could be applied to not only a parable but to everything in the gospel as well. The Gospels, Mark, Matthew, Luke, and John are in a sense *out to get us!* They are tellings meant to throw us off-kilter, to make us wonder *what if*, and to call us to conversion and a change of heart and action.

In the last chapter we looked at three parables, including the Prodigal Son, also known as the Prodigal Father, the Merciful Father, the Lost Son, or the Lost Sons. I'd like to look at the parable once more with you, this time not only looking at the individual characters and their relationships, but crucial to the parable is the concept of community and reconciliation, so let's dig more deeply into the layers, here, at something few readers explore—how the story of the two brothers is core to the parable.

All the various titles of the story reveal an aspect of the story; they deal primarily with the middle of the story, not the beginning or the end. And the beginning and the end of parables are especially the places of power and deepest insight. They are jumping-off points for being drawn deeper into the story.

In the last chapter, we looked at the three stories of Jesus, the triad, each drawing on elements of the others, and the last of the triad drawing the elements of the Lost

Sheep and the Lost Coin together. Recall that these stories are told in the context of a public feast, a shared meal. Those celebrating and eating with Jesus are people the scribes and Pharisees judge that he *shouldn't* be seen with, let alone eating with—tax collectors and sinners—outcasts and folks on the fringe of acceptable, religious society. Luke sets it up starkly:

> Tax collectors and sinners were all drawing near to listen to Jesus, but, the Pharisees and scribes began to complain, saying, "This man welcomes sinners and eats with them." So to them, Jesus addressed this parable. (Luke 15:1–3)

Keep in mind, then, as noted in the previous chapter, that the story is directed—like an arrow to the heart—to those criticizing his behavior and his dinner companions, those who self-righteously refused to join them for the meal.

Thinking in terms of community, we see, first of all, the story Jesus tells is about who you eat with, or refuse to sit at table with and the judgment rendered. And then the story begins so simply—disarmingly so: "A man had two sons." We see the story differently now, in the lens of community. Now, this story isn't about "the older brother" or "the prodigal son," this is a story about two sons of the one father. It reveals the father's relationship with both of them, and just as important, or even more so, their relationship with each other as his children.

And we know from hearing the story so often that they

both have broken relationships with their father, and as brothers they are estranged from each other. Most people listen to the story and decide which son we are like: the one who wants his inheritance now (in effect saying to the father, "I want you dead and gone") or the one who describes himself as the pleaser ("I've slaved for you my whole life"), the one who despises his father as well, but refrains from showing it in an outward way. He, too, is waiting for his father to die so he can inherit as well.

What we often forget, or are unaware of, is that in the time of Jesus, the elder son would be in a legal position to inherit everything from his father. And it was the elder son who was responsible to care for the other members of the family, carry on his father's name, and honor him. Usually, after the initial inheritance, the elder son would give a portion of the inheritance to the other children.

That the younger son wants his share now upsets the standard cultural story. And from the very first action the father takes, things start to get *strange*. Instead of following the tradition of the Jewish community, the father splits the inheritance in half and gives the younger son an equal share. From the first, Jesus's hearers would be shocked. What kind of Jew, what kind of father, is this man?

From the onset, though, the actions of the Father focus on one thing–which only becomes more obvious toward the end of the story: he is intent on getting his children to not only realize how much he loves them as his beloved children, but he acts in such a way as to unite beloved brothers/siblings into their family.

Again, we've looked at the gist of the parable. The younger son takes his share of the property and he goes off and squanders it *in dissolute living*, a description that leaves open various interpretations. What he did was sell his portion of the estate—a piece of the promised land—cutting his ties not only to his father and family, but to his race, his country, and his God.

And then the younger son falls on hard times, reduced to the lowest level of survival. He's taking care of swine—for a Jew, an abomination to be near an unclean animal. He's so hungry and miserable he wants to eat the pig slop, but nobody offers him any. He *comes to his senses*—his stomach gets to him, and thinking of himself and how to allay his hunger, he comes up with his plan.

Some interpret this change as repentance. But it is nothing of the sort. It's a coldly calculated plan to take care of his basic needs. He will return home, do what is necessary, *eat humble pie* with his father, make *nice*, and offer to work on what's left of his brother's portion of the estate. He'll get paid as a hired hand. This would rankle his brother to no end—first he loses half his inheritance, and then when his wayward brother returns, he will have to pay him while he stays at home and eats the food of the household! Insult to injury.

Off the younger, hungry one, goes. He knows he will not have it easy. When he sold his birthright and inheritance, he betrayed his community, his religion, and his God. On his route back, he will have to face not only his family, but his angry neighbors and the larger Jewish community. He's prepared. They will probably throw dung and garbage at him, if not stones. But he is desperate.

Small communities at the time shared a geography that followed the same pattern. The houses were in the heart of the town; the next layer contained the public areas, marketplaces, the well, synagogue, and other buildings; finally, there were the outlying fields owned by all the extended families. He would have to work his way back into his father's house from the center of the community.

In fact, that is the reason why his father goes out every day to seek his lost son, hoping against hope that he will return for whatever reason. If he does, the father will serve as his protective shield as soon as he appears. He'll walk back into the house with him. The father is willing to humiliate himself day after day, hoping his son returns. This action reveals what has been going on in the household—before the younger one left. The elder son held the responsibility of keeping the family together. It was the older son who should have gone after his brother or looked for him. But he disregards the most important of elder son duties, pushing his father to be further humiliated daily in front of the whole community.

The younger man returns, ready with his canned confession, but his father is a couple of steps ahead of him. He is the one who "catches sight of him from afar off, is filled with compassion, runs to him and embraces and kisses him," cutting off his speech. His father ignores what he is saying and instead, orders the servants "to quickly bring the finest robe for him; put the ring on his finger and sandals for his feet. And then take the fatted calf, slaughter it and set up a feast."

And once again, this father breaks every tradition and rule within the family and society. There is one robe—for the one who inherits it all, the signet ring that bears the seal of the family and one pair of sandals for contact in public with others in the community. Not only is he welcoming him back—he is extending all of the other son's expected authority and power as the head of the family to the younger son. It would have been the talk of the town! And it would have engendered even more anger in the eldest son.

Yet, we return to the father, to understand that he sees community wholeness in the core of the story: "Then let us celebrate with a feast, because this son of mine was dead, and has come to life again; he was lost, and has been found." And the celebration begins—the gathering of people, the telling of the story, the preparation of food, music, the entertainment, and the hard work of setting the table. The father starts the work of community in concentric circles. Phase one of the father's intentions are now set in motion.

He now deals with the elder brother's relationship (or lack of it) with himself as the father as well as his brother all this time. The older son is out in the fields, tending to what's left of his inheritance, unaware that he's lost even more then he thinks, including what he expects is still to come to him on his father's death—the robe, the ring, the sandals, and his place in the community.

And then he hears the music, the dancing, and celebration and grabs one of the servants and tries to find out what is going on. In this gospel, Luke slips servants into many of his stories, scenes, and images, reminding us it is always Jesus, the obedient servant of the Father—the actual oldest brother—who is here to preach the Good News of forgiveness. So here the servant announces to the older brother, "Your brother has returned and your father has slaughtered the fattened calf, because he has him back safe and sound." The servant is the one who proclaims the gospel!

Enraged, the older brother refuses to enter his own house. Their father went out again and again waiting for his younger son to return; now in sight of all the village, he humbles himself and goes out again to the fields, trying to lure his other son back into the house. One was lost in the *wilds* of the world out there, and this older resentful one is "lost in his father's house," in the words of Joe Silva preaching on the parable.

We now come to see how broken this relationship is between the oldest son and his father and with his younger brother. So, when his father begs him to come and welcome his brother home and join the family, bringing them together again, the son bluntly tells his father all he held inside and never spoke:

> "Look, all these years I slaved for you and not once did I disobey your orders; yet you never even gave me a kid goat to feast on with my friends. But when your son returns after swallowing up your property

with prostitutes, for him you slaughter the fattened calf." (Luke 15:29–30)

The son sees himself as a slave to his father, obeying his orders, utterly divorced from him. He refuses to acknowledge that he has a brother. In the words he uses, he only admits that his father has another son. And the father makes clear that he sees the eldest as a beloved son. And he sees his younger son as a beloved son. He sees them as brothers to one another. "My son, you are here with me always; everything I have is yours. But now we must celebrate and rejoice, because *your brother* was dead and has come to life again; he was lost and has been found."

And the story suddenly stops. The story begins when the speaker stops talking. Now it begins in the community; the story is told to the good folks who won't eat with the *others*, both beloved by Jesus, both invited to the community table. The story begins with those of us who are intent on not sharing the table, the Body of Christ, on sharing his company with others, even at Eucharist.

As with any parable, we see a few possibilities for endings to the story: Perhaps the elder brother comes back in with his father and embraces his brother–reconciled with him. Perhaps he comes back in and acts like everything is all right in front of the neighbors, while despising his brother, biding his time as he's done before, until he gets what he thinks he deserves. Perhaps he refuses to come in and instead stays in the field, shaming his father further. Perhaps then the younger brother notices they are both missing and goes out and asks forgiveness of his brother. Or, perhaps he sends a servant out with a gift, asking the brother to come in and celebrate with him and the community. Or maybe he just ignores them both and selfishly thinks he's got a good thing going here. Maybe the father goes back in, weeps, and sends his servant to each of them, begging them to return home. And maybe, like in other parables, the servant is killed by those in the field. They can both go out and meet halfway. Or, others from the community can try to bring them together, working on the one they know from friendship and life.

The possibility of the story to continue, to be told by those of us living out the story in our lives, is endless in its iterations. This is the intent of the parable. A man *had* two sons who were both lost and who refuse to live as brothers, tearing the family and the community apart.

What we know about the story is what we know about community: to sit together at the table is to forgive and be forgiven, to begin to reconcile and start to live in communion as the beloved sons and daughters of God, who is intent on bringing us all home together.

All of us are all lost in many ways—both in our worlds and in our Abba's house, and we are separated from and refusing to live in peace and in communion with our brothers and sisters.

Yes, this story is about God but unfolds as about the One in whose image we are made—Father, Beloved Child, and Spirit—holding us all as one together as The Three are One. What we discover in the parable is that our relationship with our God is only as good as our relationship with one another.

As we receive the parable and live into its possible endings, perhaps these will open doors of insight and action for us as we give this story another name: the Family Reunion, the Feast Begins! Or perhaps *Time for Dinner!*

Come home children. Come sit down at the table. Let's all of us eat together. We know in our hearts that at any meal, what's on the menu isn't the prime reason why we're there–it's whom we eat with, whom we break bread with, whom we toast with, the wine we share.

Jesus's parable told at a meal reminds us that God invites everyone to the feast, and our God wants us all to be at home, reconciled, sitting around the table, rejoicing and dwelling in peace–together.

The kingdom of God is for the broken-hearted.

–Mister Rogers

INTENTION, REFLECTION, RESPONSE

God is a father to the fatherless, a mother to the motherless. God is my sister, my brother, my leader, my guide, my teacher, my comforter, my friend. God's my all in all, my everything.

—Thea Bowman, FSPA

These words of Sr. Thea speak about our God, as seen and known in everyone in our lives, and in our world. Reading this, how does this change our image of God? In the parable, the father in the story fulfills some, if not all, of these descriptions.

And are there others you can name—preacher, prophet, confronter, one who pleads—who call us to forgiveness and reconciliation? Are there situations in your life when you might be called teacher, father, mother, sister, comforter in relation to others in your family? In this role of "father," what can you do, imitating the father of the parable to facilitate reconciliation now?

> *Anger that is motivated by compassion or a desire to correct social injustice, and does not seek to harm the other person, is a good anger that is worth having.*
>
> —Dalai Lama

The father in the parable is *justifiably* angry at both his sons, yet he treats them both the same. Repeatedly he goes out to them to try to get them to reconnect with him and with each other, as brothers. He even goes out of his way, in public, to try to get them to relate to each other as brothers. In your relationships, what can you do, how can you express your anger or deep feeling, in order to rectify situations in your life?

Both brothers are angry. The younger one is angry at his father and wants what's his now, even wanting his father dead. He's angry at his older brother, too. Why do you think he's at odds with his older brother? As to the older brother, he is angry at his father for several reasons. He sees his father as a tyrant, demanding and controlling the way he lives. Then he's resentful at how his other brother is treated kindly by their father—when the younger brother displayed *bad* behavior, even as the older brother doesn't feel appreciated, even though he does what "has to" or "should do," feeding his resentment.

Who are you angry with? Why? Do you see yourself comparing how others are treated with how you perceive yourself being treated. Are you angry at others when you play the comparison game? How do you deal with your anger or resentment, seeing God loving all of us and forgiving all of us, no matter what we or anyone has done?

> *O God, we are one with You. You have made us one with You. You have taught us that if we are open to one another, You dwell in us. Help us to preserve this openness and to fight for it with all our hearts. Help us to realize that there can be no understanding where there is mutual rejection. O God, in accepting one another wholeheartedly, fully, completely, we accept You with our whole being, because our being is in Your being, our spirit is rooted in Your spirit. Fill us then with love, and let us be bound together with love as we go our diverse ways, united in this one Spirit which makes You present in the world, and which makes You witness to the ultimate reality that is love. Love has overcome. Love is victorious.*
>
> —Thomas Merton

What in this prayer do you find new, surprising, hard to pray, even distressing? After praying this prayer several times, share your reactions and responses with others. Does this prayer change how you feel about God, about others, even about yourself?

You should be angry. You must not be bitter. Bitterness is like cancer. It eats upon the host . . . so use that anger. You write it. You paint it. You dance it. You vote it. You do everything about it. You talk it. Never stop talking it.

—Maya Angelou

How do you use your anger? How can you make it creative, imaginative. How do you use it, express it, without harm or violence, with invitation and welcome to others—and with healing for your own feelings?

5

Forgiveness and Reconciliation

As long as we are on earth, the love that unites us will bring us suffering, by our very contact with one another, because this love is the resetting of a Body of broken bones.

–Thomas Merton

Not everything that is faced can be changed, but nothing can be changed until it is faced.

–James Baldwin

In Jewish thought, a sin is not an offense against God, an act of disobedience. A sin is a missed opportunity to act humanly.

–Rabbi Harold Kushner

Forgiveness and reconciliation are intimately tied together, because reconciliation is mutual forgiveness. *Reconciliation* means to walk together again. It even describes a specific kind of walking. If you have ever tried a three-legged race, you have a sense of it. Two individuals each bind one leg to the other, put their arms over each other's shoulders, and attempt to walk together.

This walking together demands a rhythm, learning the pace of the other person, and sensing their weaknesses and strength, and adjusting to the other person. Reconciliation is a learned art that takes a lot of practice. It's not just a one-time experience, but a response of working together with each person calls for a unique response, depending on the situation.

Reconciliation is the ongoing call to integrate a practice deep into our hearts, minds, and memories. In a sense reconciliation is the completing of forgiveness, an extension of forgiveness toward others, a gift shared with one another, and then with others. It's like a good *infection* that spreads, grows, and even mutates. It can be caught when experienced through others, or even when we witness or hear about the reconciliation story of other peoples' lives.

Reconciliation begins by seeking out one another, with confession, with acknowledgment, or admitting our failures and sin to another person or to our community. The first step to reconciliation is being truthful and speaking of a reality that is a part of our past, of a behavior or action that we know is impacting the present and needs to be either stopped and/or undone.

Turning from the past is part of repentance and reconciliation. In Hebrew the theological term is *teshuvah*, a turning that relies on God's being open to us always, as God desires our return to him even more strongly than we want to return to God or to the one we have wronged or separated ourselves from.

In the Jewish community the time from Rosh Hashanah to Yom Kippur focuses on this process, sourced in words from the prophet Hosea: "Return [*shuva*], O Israel, to the Lord your God, for you have fallen because of your sin. Take words with you and return [*shuvu*] to the Lord" (Hosea 14:2–3).

This period is called the Days of Awe. It is coming home to the Lord and returning to ourselves, first by accepting God's forgiveness and then turning to offer that forgiveness to others. And when this happens, it is said in the commentary *Deuteronomy Rabbah*, "that the gates of repentance are always open."

Even this first step of admitting what we have done and turning toward rectifying the situation can be incredibly difficult, as a story told in ancient Persia relates about a king who wanted to purchase a gift of fine and very expensive jewelry for his wife. He went with some of his entourage to the shop and looked through the display of rings, bracelets, and necklaces. After a while, he selected the one he decided on and had it wrapped carefully.

They left the shop and headed back to the palace. They had not gone far when the shopkeeper came running after them. Distraught, he stopped the king and said that while they were in the shop, he had been robbed. There were two priceless rings missing—someone in his company must have stolen them.

The king was upset, but he also knew that it was entirely possible that what the shopkeeper said might be true. They all headed back to the shop. And all the way back, the king thought about what to do. When they arrived and all were lined up facing the displays, the king asked the shopkeeper to find a large urn with an opening wide enough for a man to get his entire arm into it and to fill it about three quarters of the way up with fine sand. The man obeyed. The urn filled with sand was placed on a small table.

The king turned to the men with him and told them, "I'm not interested in who stole the rings or even if it was more than one of you, but I am interested in returning the items to the rightful owner. I am asking each of you to approach the urn and put one of your arms into it—up to your shoulder. If you have stolen something, please take this opportunity to conceal it in your hand and then leave it behind in the sand when you remove your arm."

All the men and the shopkeeper were surprised, but one by one they all obeyed and went forward, putting their arms into the urn, leaving them there for just a moment or two and then taking their arms back out. When all had done it, the king told the shopkeeper to empty out the sand. He did and behold, in with the sand were the two rings that had disappeared, along with two small pins (or brooches).

Relieved, the shopkeeper enthusiastically expressed his thanks to the king. The king was shamed and disappointed with his men, expressing how he felt, but also told them he was grateful that they returned the stolen property and so proved their honesty, even if belated, and after the fact.

The story spread quickly through the city and other merchants. When the king was asked why he came up with this *ruse* to get them to return the stolen items, he said that he wanted to make it as easy as possible for whoever had taken the items to do the right thing and replace what they had taken to its rightful owner.

There are ways to reconcile our actions with justice in forgiveness and reconciliation. And the process of restitution begins by replacing and restoring what has been damaged or harmed. This is restorative justice, the next step in extending forgiveness and reconciling with one another. In this step all those involved in doing evil, committing sin, begin to undo the harm that has been done to others.

One story in scripture, from Luke's Gospel, shows us how Jesus forgives, reconciles, and teaches us how to begin to do restitution, living out a way to restore, initiating holiness and wholeness after destroying and harming others and so disobeying God.

The story begins with the disciple Peter (Luke 22) when the soldiers, palace servants, and bystanders are in the courtyard waiting while Jesus is arraigned before his trial.

First, as Peter mingles with others in the courtyard,

he is accused of being associated with *the Nazarene* by a serving maid of the high priest. He denies it, saying, "I don't know what you are talking about." Then a second time, the serving maid talks now to the bystanders around Peter, accusing him again, saying, "you are one of them." Again, he denies it strongly.

Later one of the bystanders says to Peter, "You are one of them, you are a Galilean." This time Peter begins to curse and swear that he does not even know Jesus. He vehemently disassociates himself from any connection with Jesus.

"Then Peter remembered the word that Jesus had said to him," we read in the text, "Before the cock crows twice you will deny me three times." Peter breaks down and weeps (Luke 22:54–62). He has severed his relationship with Jesus in the presence of others who witness Peter's betrayal.

A story in John 21 offers a response to this experience of Peter's betrayal. It is found in a resurrection appearance story that has three parts: in the first portion, called the Great Catch, we see the disciples out fishing on the Sea of Tiberius. They catch sight of a figure on the shore. He is recognized by the beloved disciple, who announces that it is Jesus. Jesus asks them if they have caught anything. They yell back that they have caught nothing.

From the shore Jesus tells them where to fish. They place their nets in the new place, and haul in so many fish they have trouble getting the net to the shore. Simon Peter puts on his clothes and jumps into the water heading toward the shore to meet Jesus, who tells him to bring some of the fish just caught.

The second story is Breakfast on the Beach, and opens with Jesus tending a fire, baking bread, and cooking the fish Peter brought to him. He serves the disciples, and they are silent, saying nothing in this very quiet and awkward breakfast with Jesus as their servant. It is Eucharist. And in the breaking of the bread, all are forgiven.

The third story follows when they have finished breakfast. Jesus asks Simon Peter to walk with him along the shore and they *walk together again*, talking.

> When they had finished breakfast, Jesus said to Simon Peter, "Simon, son of John, do you love me more than these?" He said to him, "Yes, Lord, you know that I love you." He said to him, "Feed my lambs." He said to him a second time, "Simon, son of John, do you love me?" He said to him, "Yes, Lord, you know that I love you." He said to him, "Tend my sheep." He said to him a third time, "Simon, son of John, do you love me?" Peter was distressed that he had said to him a third time, "Do you love me? and he said to him, "Lord, you know everything; you know that I love you." Jesus said to him, "Feed my sheep." (John 21:15–17)

There is another segment of the story that continues with Jesus's words to Simon Peter regarding his future and his death, ending with the command he began with: "Follow me."

The crucified and risen Jesus speaks with Simon bar Jonah, the name Peter was known by before following Jesus and being given his name, *Peter*, by Jesus. This is a ritual encounter between the two, with levels of meaning in each of the three questions and answers.

First Jesus asks, "Do you love me more than these?" There are many expressions and depth of love among the disciples, and with us. It is a formal question, as Jesus uses both names: Simon and Peter.

Peter answers simply: "Yes, Lord, you know that I love you."

Each answer to each question from Jesus echoes in the excuses Simon Peter gave those in the courtyard who accused him of simply *knowing* Jesus. The word *love* in Jesus's question is *agape*, a deep and abiding love of a friend and a disciple. But the word Simon Peter uses to answer is love–*philo*–a term of basic affection that sometimes verges on friendship. And Jesus answers: "Feed my lambs." Not exactly the response we'd expect, unless we think of Jesus as the Good Shepherd seeking the one that has left the flock. "Feed my sheep," Jesus says to Simon Peter: to *feed*, is to nourish, to give sustenance, and to sustain the life of the least of his brothers and sisters, the other disciples and members of the flock. This command includes providing the basic needs of water, food, shelter, pasture, protection, and security. Some say this command to Peter suggests he is to admit his own dismal failures to his community and make sure they all know how he denied Jesus in his time of need, as Peter pulled away from him at a crucial juncture. New Christians and believers need to know Peter's sin and his disbelief, even after he had been following Jesus for some time.

Then the second time, in the same question from Jesus to Simon Peter, Jesus uses the same word for love: *agape*. And this time Peter answers using the same words: "Yes, Lord, you know that I love you."

There is an established relationship between Jesus, his disciple, who, along with the other disciples, Jesus called his friends, if they obey him and make his words come true in their lives. This time, Jesus responds with the command, "Tend my sheep." To tend, as a shepherd does, means keeping the sheep together, herding them, attending to their needs in their environment, even going after the lost and straying ones, the drifting ones, and those who for other reasons are on the fringes—the sick, infirm, and distraught. When we remember the lost sheep and the other ninety-nine in the field, we hear this second command as the next penance Simon Peter must put into practice.

A third time, the question is posed. And Simon Peter, we are told, is *distressed* that Jesus would ask him three times. Remember the scene in the courtyard and how *distressed* Jesus was when he was betrayed. Simon Peter doesn't seem to register that he is being given the threefold chance to undo the harm he has done, in hurting Jesus and in the terrible example he gave to the other disciples and all those who witnessed what was happening. This time the word Jesus returns to is the one that Simon Peter keeps using: *philo*. Jesus accommodates him, seeking to lead him back closer to him, and to the other disciples, hoping he will grow, change, and be converted to the kind of love Jesus has for him and for all of us.

Like most of us, Peter is slow to learn and change, something that will change when Jesus later speaks to him about the future and what his life, and death, will be, when he knows the cross. But in this moment of questions, Peter's love is still tentative.

Now Jesus's command is "Feed my sheep": Simon Peter's third penance. He has to undo the harm and reconnect and reconcile with others and with God. This is restorative justice that entails forgiveness: forgive all no matter what, all the time, with inclusion, as Jesus did in sharing Eucharist with all of them, no strings attached.

Feed first and then talk later and deal with what needs to be attended to. For now, Peter is to forgive others as he has been forgiven by Jesus, especially if it involves others, in public, and those who are leaders in the community. The more power the person has, the more public is the reconciling and restoring required for communion and unity. Peter and others are to reach out to others, and not wait for others to return or come to them, and Peter certainly is not to do anything that impedes their return.

How gracious Jesus is with Simon Peter, confronting him for what he did and failed to do, for his betrayal, denying him, even cursing him. He does this by inviting Peter to avow his love for him three times.

Any experience of forgiveness is meant to become reconciliation and then restoration. This restorative justice is never just between us and God, or even just between one another. It involves others, the whole community coming together, with everyone mindful of what they have done, and failed to do, and how it affects everyone else.

In Jewish tradition, there is a story often told on the feast of Yom Kippur about returning and finding our way back home, back to God and to the community. This is the way I heard it: Once upon a time there was a young woman who lived on the edge of a vast forest. People rarely entered it for fear of wild animals or who might live there. The young woman loved the edge of the great trees, the vast greenery and the smell of such life and freshness, and so she walked often just along the edge and a few feet inside beside the great trees and lush ground cover of roots, ferns, and vegetation. One afternoon she was very upset at something that had happened and went to walk off her anger and hurt. It took longer than usual, and without noticing it, she moved further into the forest, becoming absorbed in the different trees, wildflowers, fledging trees. And as she was enchanted, she forgot her feelings, relaxed, and breathed easier. It was a good while before she realized there was less and less sunlight and the shadows had grown longer and darker.

She turned to go home and within moments, she realized she had lost her bearings and was very lost, having no idea of direction or how deep she had wandered. In the darkening she finally found a tree with a large hole, and she curled up to spend the night. It was a long one and she slept fitfully. But as dawn came and the light penetrated deep into the woods, she set out to find her way home.

She wandered all day, chewed on some berries, and found a stream with fresh water, but she did not find her way out. Again, she spent another night, half sleeping, waking at every sound.

She began to think she needed to find food, and make some sort of a lean-to shelter, and start seriously searching for a way out. For days and nights, this was her life. She would mark where she was and calculate in which direction she went, noting anything that might be food, always aware of water and anything that would afford her shelter. As the days continued, she started marking trees and remembering what day it was as well as where she was. And she was afraid that she'd never find her way out.

Weeks had gone by, and one day she heard noises and realized it was another person somewhere nearby. She hid and watched and found a young man making his way through the woods, looking at everything very intently. He had heard her presence, too. Finally, she came and stood beside a tree, and he stopped, too, and they looked at each other. He began first, saying, "Please, don't leave. I won't hurt you; I'm sorry I frightened you. I am lost."

She responded, saying, "I'm lost, too," and blurted out what she knew about where she was and how long it had been and that she was afraid she'd never find her way out. They shared their food and water that evening and talked about what to do. Neither of them knew where *out* or home was or which direction to head off in the next morning. But after a long quiet, one of them said, "You don't know how to go home, and I don't know how to go home, but both of us know which directions not to go in–where we're already been and failed."

Their hope was renewed, and together they decided they would seek to return home and share all they had with each other on the way.

This story tells us so much about the inner landscape of our lives. But more than anything, it tells us we are all the same, looking to return home and that we are together on the way.

We seek God, we seek to live with grace and freedom and to share what we have with one another. We even come to realize that perhaps where we are now is home and that if, on occasion, we are lost and mistake what we do and where we go, we can still live, because we are always forgiven for everything, we are reconciled with God and with one another. And together we can restore our lives and make our way together.

The way to right wrongs is to turn the light of truth upon them.

–Ida B. Wells-Barnett

Forgiveness is simply understanding that every one of us is both inherently good and inherently flawed, within every hopeless situation and every seemingly hopeless person lies the possibility of transformation.

—Archbishop Desmond Tutu

In the event of the insufficiency of everything attainable we come to understand that here, in this life, all symphonies remain unfinished.

—Karl Rahner, SJ

INTENTION, REFLECTION, RESPONSE

We are all flawed human beings. But it helps to regularly look at ourselves honestly and admit our sins, failures, and shortcomings. Even as we know, as the James Baldwin quote at the beginning of this chapter states, "Not everything that is faced, can be changed. But nothing can be changed until it is faced." What do you need to face right now? What is one thing you'd like to work at changing?

Jesus asks Simon Peter three times: "Do you love me?" and each time Peter answers, "Yes," though his yes is a bit different each time. How often do you say these words: Lord, I love you? Or how often do you say (if only just to yourself), that you love the people in your life, including the ones you are *at odds with* or angry with or need to reconcile with?

Consider, right now, are there people you need to reconcile with—to walk together with again? It can be a single person, or a group, someone from your past or very present to you. Even though Simon Peter was estranged from Jesus, Jesus began with something very positive, inviting, and welcoming in his question of "Do you love me?" What can you say to open a conversation that seeks to reconcile someone to you? If you are in a group setting, share these suggestions with others. Wisdom is found in sharing your story and wisdom with others gathered who are dealing with the same feelings and needs.

Some of us, when we were children, played a game that often started when we found ourselves with a great number of daisies around. We'd take a flower and begin to take the petals off. With each one, we'd say, "he loves me, he loves me not" or "she loves me, she loves me not." Mostly we were waiting to end with the last remaining petal and the words, she/he loves me! Yes, it is a child's game, but to use that metaphor on people who are a part of your life and who are not in that "love" category, it can help us to do this as a ritual, reminding us of how God loves us, all of us, and that this is what we are called to with all others.

A story was told during the Civil War when the South was still fighting the North over the issue of slavery. Someone asked Lincoln, "When this war is over, how are you going to treat those who fought us, when they are conquered and have to rejoin the Union? They're our enemies—how are you going to deal with them?" Lincoln's answer was simple: "I'm going to treat them as if they had never been away." How do you feel about Lincoln's answer? Are there occasions when that is precisely how we feel called to treat some of the people who have wronged us—much the same way Jesus treats Simon Peter?

"Reconciliation is not a simple affair," wrote Blessed Pierre Claverie, a Dominican in Algeria, later killed with his Muslim driver by a car bomb in 1996. "It comes at a high price. It can also involve, as it did for Jesus, being torn apart between irreconcilable opposites. . . . So, then, what's the choice? Well, Jesus does not choose. He says, in effect, 'I love you all,' and he dies" (*A Life Poured Out: Pierre Claverie of Algeria*).

What are the situations in the world today that you or groups you belong to are involved in, where you find yourself in this kind of torn-apart situation? Do you as an individual or these groups as communities need to reconcile in a choice to love all?

"If you believe that Jesus Christ is Lord to the glory of God the Father in the power of the Holy Spirit, then all the way home to heaven is heaven," wrote Catherine of Siena (*The Dialogue of Saint Catherine of Siena*).

Reflecting on this quote, do you believe this? What does it mean for your daily life?

6

Reconciliation and Restorative Justice

Justice is what love looks like in public.

—Cornel West

Silence in the face of evil is itself evil. God will not hold us guiltless. Not to speak is to speak. Not to act is to act.

—Dietrich Bonhoeffer

For forgiveness to become reconciliation—which is mutual forgiveness—it is necessary for us to change, to seek to undo the harm that has been done, to make recompense for wrongs, to do restitution. This change of restorative justice traditionally has been called *penance* in the church. Over time penance became more about prayers to recite. But penance is action. It is righting what is wrong. It is being converted, interrupting and changing reality and replacing what was done and its harmful effects with goodness. The action of penance is working to return to wholeness, to rebalance and to restore humanity.

Penance is restorative justice. And it is an action both singular (one to one), but it is intimately connected to everyone: those involved on the perimeters of the experience, and all those who are impacted by what has happened and their reactions and responses. It reveals that every single action affects everyone, moving far beyond anything the original individuals were aware of—out into the universe.

This sounds impossible, but in reality, our actions reverberate. Many can attest to how one action can affect far-flung situations and many people. Knowing this broadens our perspectives and reveals how closely we are bound to one another.

I first heard a story called "The Agreement" by Barry Lopez, but after retelling it several times among Indigenous peoples, they corrected me. The actual title is "Covenants."

It was once upon a time, and it was long ago, long before any people were living in this valley in northwestern Canada and the US. There were bears . . . lots of them. And there were salmon . . . lots of them. There was the river from and to the sea that was the salmon's highway home, and it stretched up into the country of the bears. The bears loved the salmon and depended on them for their food.

Now the bears and the salmon had an agreement: the bears would only take what they needed to eat, so that the salmon could make their way upriver to spawn, and so survive, and there would be another season and more salmon. This is the way it was—in fact, this is the way it was with just about everything. There were agreements, and that's the way things lived and thrived and survived from season to season and from year to year.

Though the bears had made an agreement with the salmon, neither the bears nor the salmon had made an agreement with the river. Every year, the salmon came in from the deep ocean and tore up the river in the thousands, hundreds of thousands, fighting the currents, heading exhausted to their spawning grounds, to their home, to their death. One year, though, when the salmon arrived, the river pulled back and the salmon were left panting and gasping on the beach until the tide came in. They tried again and again. It was autumn, and it was necessary for the salmon to get upriver before it was too late.

Eventually, there were words, a lot of them, between the river and the salmon. But there was no agreement. Finally, the river decided to let the salmon come in and upriver. The river was packed with the salmon struggling upstream. Then the salmon arrived in the country of the bears, who were hungry and waiting impatiently for them.

Suddenly the river went wild. It went backward in one direction and forward in another, with boulders and rocks all over and spumes of white water and the banks all rocky. The bears were terrified and hid behind the trees. The salmon didn't know what to do.

Then the river stopped, and all was quiet. Nothing moved, and nothing was said. Then the river spoke, saying it needed an agreement, just like the one that had existed between the bears and the salmon. It was tired of being ignored and taken for granted, and only noticed when it was thought to be useful.

So, the salmon and the river talked for days. The salmon explained who they were and where they came from, and what it was like to fight their way upriver to home, to spawn and die. And the bears talked about who they were, about their long sleep and how hungry they were, and how they needed to feed their young cubs; they said that the salmon were delicious and nutritious and they couldn't live without them. Then the river talked about where it came from, and how it went down to the sea and how it knew the seasons, and the birds and the otters; it told of how it had agreements with the wind and the rain and all the different kinds of fish that lived in it or used it to travel home.

They talked about what they needed and what they'd give in exchange. They talked, and they listened for a long time. And then, quite unexpectedly, the river said something no one had ever said before or ever heard before. The river said it loved the salmon, and it waited for their coming every year. Those words changed everything. This was truth. This was trust. This was the basis of a strong and powerful agreement, and everyone was very pleased. So, they each went their own way, connected now to each other.

You think this is a story, but it's not–it's reality. It's the way things are and have been since the beginning. Life is all about agreements. You can't just take what you want and ignore others. You can't just live independent of others. Everyone has agreements—everyone, that is except humans—two-leggeds.

What season of the year is it now? Go outside and watch, feel—you will get a sense of all the agreements, between birds and winter, when to stay and when to go and to return. You will feel them on your skin and breathe them in and out. Stand on the earth in your bare feet; then enter the water and feel its energy and how it swirls around you. Breathe and lift your face to the skies.

It is said among the old ones and those who know the language of the trees that it is only humans who do not honor the agreements; they don't even think to make them anymore. They take everything for granted and are so greedy and destructive. They do not even honor the common courtesies anymore, and so they keep breaking the heart of the Great Spirit. Can you hear the Great Spirit crying, moaning, and aching across the world and through the skies?

Covenants are agreements entered into before the Creator, who will demand an accounting of every creature's faithfulness. According to their story, the animals, birds, and earth want to be witnesses when the Creator brings human beings before the Great Spirit to give an account of what they have done and been for the earth. They want to be there to listen and see justice done—finally.

Each of us, all of us, must strive to be aware of our connection to other human beings, to realize and live bound to the human family, to the earth and all the worlds we make and dwell in, and the universe we exist within.

This is especially true when we are confronted with or caught up in the consequences that are evil, unjust, violent, and destructive. And we must continue to relate to those who have broken faith or dishonored the covenants that bind us all as one together.

In John's Gospel there is a resurrection story of Jesus appearing within a gathering, even though the doors to the room are locked. He breaks into where his followers are gathered, holding their fear after the events of the crucifixion. This story is core to what resurrection life is the Trinity, and to each other. Jesus's words to those in the room—and to us—are the basis of living life in his Spirit and with him with us in the world.

> On the evening of that first day of the week, when the doors were locked, where the disciples were, for fear of the Jews, Jesus came and stood in their midst and said to them: "Peace be with you." When he had said this, he showed them his hands and his side. The disciples rejoiced when they saw the Lord. Jesus said to them again: "Peace be with you. As the Father has sent me, so I send you." And when he had said this, he breathed on them, "Receive the Holy Spirit. Whose sins you forgive, they are forgiven them, and whose sins you retain, they are retained." (John 20:19–24)

As they are huddled in fear and confusion, they are given a gift of the Risen Lord breaking into the room of all of us, offering the gift of his heart.

Huddled in fear, hiding from all the other people in Jerusalem: the Romans, all the visitors that came for the Passover, most of the Jewish people, and their own families and neighbors. Into their hiding and fear Jesus comes and stands in their midst.

One time, as I was telling this story, a young man, maybe twelve or thirteen years old, wildly waved his hand at me, trying to get my attention. He stood up and boldly explained to me and to everyone, "Hey, he's come back from the dead, and is alive. He's God. He just rearranged his molecules and slipped through." After a stunned silence, then a good bit of laughter, the group got to thinking. The young man revealed the wisdom of such a radical shift in Jesus's body that hinted at its power and effects on everything because the resurrection affects everything. Everyone.

Jesus's words repeated three times are the proclamation of resurrection: "Peace be with you"–*shalom*–the traditional greeting among the Jews, also adopted by Christians from the very beginnings of the faith. Four simple words in English. They are not only a greeting, they are a blessing, a hoped-for reality, a gift.

But perhaps even more, the words are a demand, a command. This peace is the presence of the Risen Lord and now our life force, our energy, the grace that moves our lives and binds us together in God as one.

Peace be with you is the first of the three peace benedictions. The first, many say, is the Peace of the Father. The second is the Peace of Jesus the crucified and Risen Lord. And the last, coming later in the account, when Jesus meets again with the gathered, is the Peace of the Spirit.

The peace of the Father is the peace of Genesis, the peace of creation that is seeded in all that has been made by the word and breath of God. It is wholeness, holiness, life that is still evolving, mutating, and becoming, that continues as Creator and Maker God still creating as "in the beginning." Now this peace announces the life force of Jesus's rising from the dead, life ever new and transforming, rebirthing and transfiguring all peoples, all worlds, and all the earth.

Jesus accompanies these words as he shows those gathered his hands and his side where his wounds scar his body, reminding them of all he suffered, the violence, the trauma, the brutality, and the inhumanity that sought to obliterate him in death.

These death-defying marks enforce his words: undoing all evil, all harm, all violence, injustice, suffering, and death itself. The gathered disciples and others initially react to him with ecstatic rejoicing. They are beside themselves with sheer exuberance and delight. But Jesus wants to bring them back to the reality of the resurrected one standing with them, human and alive despite what has happened. So, again he speaks the words: Peace be with you. When we hear the phrase the first time, we hear the emphasis of the first word: *Peace.*

Now as Jesus says the words a second time, the emphasis can be placed on the word *be*. It is a command, demand, and creates his presence, his power, his energy, his grace, and re-creates them—and us—in his image, the image of the crucified and risen person in their midst, among us.

As from this emphasis of peace comes an extension of his command of mission: "As the Father has sent me, so I send you." Often the word *now* is inserted into translations, so the force of Jesus's words comes through focused on this as life from now on. "So now I send you."

Before we are sent to live in purpose, we meet the peace of Jesus, the Word and the flesh of God incarnate, who is like us, with us, all ways. And now our lives belong to him; we live not only with him but for him. We live to incarnate his Word, his presence in our own lives, and share that life with others, following the example he gave. He came that "we might have life and have it ever more abundantly" (John 11). Now we are to live from that restorative peace, sharing that with everyone else, so that they can live ever more abundantly as well.

After Jesus spoke the word of peace and mission, he *breathed on them*. This is Genesis quantum-leaped into our existence now. Once more God breathes into each one of us, re-creating us in his image, the image of the Lord, suffering, dying, and rising. And Jesus speaks once more, with his next words instructing us on how to live and share his grace and life with others: "Receive the Holy Spirit." This is the promised gift from the Father now handed over to us—breathed into our bodies, souls, minds, hearts, and spirits, *inspiriting* us—as Teilhard de Chardin would describe how God inhabits and dwells in us now by the mysterious gift of the Incarnation, God becoming human with us.

All that we have spoken of and sought to take to heart as the Good News of forgiveness is confirmed. This is what the Spirit is given for: "Whose sins you forgive are forgiven them" (John 20:23). Forgiveness, we discover, is part of the air we breathe, the inhaling and exhaling, the way we communicate and connect, even participate in communion with one another as God does.

What comes next as the second part of the gift of the Spirit's life and power are words that bind us to others: "And whose sins you retain are retained" (John 20:23). But looking at the original language, the words more accurately read: "And whose sins you hold bound are held bound." Where forgiveness is being loosed, set free, the other side of this is to be held bound. This word only appears twice in John's Gospel, used again in the story of Lazarus being raised from the dead.

The gospel story relates how Lazarus has died and has been buried, his body bound in burial cloths, wrapped and enshrouded, round and round, as a mummy would be contained and enclosed. When he is summoned forth by the sound of the Word of God, from the tomb, Lazarus comes out—as his body most probably was standing upright in the narrow confines of the rock tomb, still bound in cloths, falling out onto the ground. The gospel reads: "The dead man came out, tied hand and foot with burial bands, and his face was wrapped in a cloth. So, Jesus said to them, "Untie him and let him go" (John 11:44).

Again these words untie him and let him go are better rendered *unbind* him and *set him free.* Jesus instructs those—his community surrounding him—to finish the work of bringing Lazarus back from the dead and into life again.

Those who obeyed and released Lazarus from his binding cloths were most probably the same women who prepared Lazarus's naked body for burial. His sisters and friends would have moved and unwrapped him from the bonds that held his body together, and then they would have helped him to stand upright before Jesus. They unwrap him from the bonds of death, raising him to stand before Jesus.

Jesus commands us *to forgive* and gives us the responsibility *to hold bound.* Rarely do we hear about or consider this, let alone do so in reality. To hold someone bound is to keep them inert, to keep them from continuing to do what they were doing, to stop them; and in this case, binding stops people from enacting sin, evil, injustice, violence, all that harms us and all others. This is Jesus's agreement, his covenant with us now—to forgive and set free all who want to live *in the freedom of the children of God*—which you'll recall are words from our baptismal promises. But we also hold bound those who do evil and harm others.

We are not adept at holding others bound, holding them accountable for the evil and harm they have done—and we don't take well to others holding us bound, stopping us from harms we perpetrate. Yet, this is God's way of doing justice. In Jesus, we are blessed in peace, freed to live, gifted with the grace and power of the Spirit of the Risen Lord.

This is the practice of restorative justice, the art and spirituality of undoing the harm that has been done, stopping the evil and redeeming the consequences of our destructive actions and words.

Those three commands of Jesus to Simon Peter were his penance—how Peter was to live the rest of his life reclaiming Jesus's way in his own person, proclaiming in his body and life the Good News to the Poor, Jesus's Gospel: his way, his truth, and his life. This is how Simon Peter was to make amends for his past life and betrayals and turn again into following Jesus.

With the power of the Spirit of the Risen Lord we are to not only forgive but to hold others bound to the Word of God to live lives that are human, holy, compassionate, and loving of others in the reciprocal spirit of Jesus's words: "as I your God love you." Forgiving is hard. And being held bound by others and holding others bound from harming others, as individuals and in community, is hard, too.

But we are not alone in this compassionate loving. The Spirit guides us in the work of community wholeness and restorative justice. When Jesus speaks that third "Peace be with you" to those who are gathered a week later, now including Thomas, Jesus breaks into the locked room again, speaking these words to the gathered, now including Thomas, the peace extends to *more.* After Jesus's first appearance to them, the other disciples told Thomas of seeing the Risen Lord, of his words and breath upon them, of giving them his Spirit. Thomas refused to believe them.

So, when Jesus gave the third command of peace to Thomas and those who gathered, before they were sent out into the world, as the Father sent Jesus, we hear the emphasis change once more: "Peace be *with you*"—the peace of the Spirit that demands that Thomas—and all of us—listen and obey.

Jesus holds Thomas bound, insisting that he not only believe his words but the other disciples' words. The words Jesus says to Thomas are "do not be unbelieving" or best translated, "do not persist in your unbelief."

We often talk about Thomas doubting, but Jesus's assessment of Thomas's actions suggest he is selfishly and stubbornly refusing to be a disciple and demands outrageous and insensitive expressions before he changes his ways. He demands a violent and callous criterion to make him believe: to tear open Jesus's healed-over wounds and make them bleed again. The name *Thomas, Didymous* means "twin," specifically identical twin. Some believe that the reason he's absent from the group in the first place is that he is betraying Jesus, leaving the disciples, and going off on his own. Maybe he has been stating that he does not even know Jesus, and others who question him have him confused with his twin. It would have been a convenient way of excusing his absence and his betrayal of his Master, Jesus. Perhaps Jesus is holding him bound for what he does and the effect it has on all the other disciples and their families. Thomas single-handedly stops Jesus's Word from being preached and given to others—so a week later, the ones who gather are still living in fear, and Jesus has to come to them yet again.

Telling the truth, binding Thomas to the truth, as Jesus does to Thomas, is the work of justice, and what restorative justice is, and shows us how justice works. It is one on one, but more often, practiced in community, with others. And this is something we'll look at in the next chapter, as we see Jesus address Thomas, in the presence of others, thus beginning the process of righting the wrong, undoing the harm inflicted, and opening a way into life-giving, creative, and imaginative ways of re-creating or restoring life, relationships and others' battered hearts and souls.

In this context of how we are to live, both forgiving others and holding them bound, in the power of the Spirit of the Risen Lord, we close with an old story from England. It is a simple story, a parable, that leaves us to finish not only the story but how we will live from now on, as followers of the Risen Lord of our lives who is both forgiving and holding us bound.

Once upon a time, there was an old man. He lived at the outskirts of the village, apart from all others. He lived simply, with a garden of flowers, herbs, and food, and he rarely left his home. But the neighborhood children wondered who he was really and why he lived on the edge of town, not participating in their daily life.

Some children said they heard their parents say he had done something terrible and was in exile, and so they feared him. Others said he was once very wealthy but had lost everything, and that's why he lived so poorly. Others said he was a wise man, a hermit who was known far and wide but lived near them in silence and reflection.

Inevitably, the young children would come and spy on him, looking to find out something about him. And there were some who tormented him: they pulled up his vegetables, trampled his flowers and herbs, left dead birds and animals and dung on his doorstep. They would throw stones at his windows and yell at him, and then run away. He never yelled back and never spoke to their parents about what the children were doing.

One of the ringleaders of the group of children, a young boy, hatched a plan and talked all of them into being a part of it. He wanted to shame the old man and prove to them that he was just useless—as well the boy wanted to prove his own power in influencing the group.

His plan was simple. He would catch a young dove and they would all go to the front door of the old man's hut and rap on it. When he answered he could stand right in front of him, with all the others behind him, backing him up and confront him. He would declare that he was holding a young dove hidden behind his back trapped in his hands. He would tell him that they all knew he wasn't wise, and they could prove it.

The old man was to decide in which hand he held the dove—his right hand or his left hand. For one held a dead bird, the other one still alive. He was to choose the hand that held the live bird if he was wise.

But what the boy planned to do was crush the bird to death no matter which hand the man chose. It was simple to do and he could do it in an instant. The others were pleased—they'd get the old man, no matter what he said.

They arrived, all of them, and rapped on the man's door. He soon answered it, standing before them. He took a moment and looked at all of them, saving his glance at the young boy at the front of the group until the end, obviously the ringleader.

He smiled at them and asked what it was they might want, and what he could do for them. The boy was quick. He set out the proposition: he had a dove in one of his hands, hidden behind his back. They wanted to know how wise he was and was the bird dead or alive. The boy kept a straight face, trying hard not to snicker or smirk.

The others were all quiet, watching to see what would happen. The old man looked at each of them in turn, ending with the boy with the bird in his hands. His face was sad but he just sighed. Then he looked the young boy for a moment and then spoke. He said solemnly, "The answer is in your hands." And just stood there.

Again, we see what storytellers the world over say: The story begins when the teller stops talking. And this is most certainly true in the case of this story. All parables throw the story, like a hot potato of our childhood games, into our lap. It is up to us to decide what to do as we react or respond.

This is the intent of the wise old man, and it is Jesus's intent in dealing with us as he preaches the Good News to the Poor. In this gospel we are told that the gift of the Spirit that comes from the mouth and hands of the Risen Lord, from our Father, does the same thing. It leaves us with the question of how we will write the ending.

In all relationships and circumstances, we must choose to forgive and set free or to resist evil, stopping it in its tracks, and hold others bound for the harm and the evil they do.

The answer is always "in our hands" as we consider how to live in wholeness with one another in our own communities and church as well as with all the people that we share our lives with on this earth.

> *My humanity is bound up with yours. For we can only be human together.*
>
> –Desmond Tutu

> *Forgiving and being reconciled to our enemies or our loved ones is not about pretending that things are other than they are. It is not about patting one another on the back and turning a blind eye to the wrong. True reconciliation exposes the awfulness, the abuse, the hurt to the truth. It could even sometimes make things worse. It is a risky undertaking but in the end it is worthwhile, because in the end only an honest confrontation with reality can bring real*

healing. Superficial reconciliation can bring only superficial healing.

–Desmond Tutu

INTENTION, REFLECTION, RESPONSE

Christian culture adjusts itself far too easily to the worship of power. In his sermons and writings, Dietrich Bonhoeffer reflected that Christians should take a stronger stand in favor of the weak, rather than considering first the possible rights of the strong. Christians should give more offense and shock the world far more than they are doing now. How do you respond to the responsibility to resist and hold others bound to and accountable for their words and actions? How does that make you feel? What's your initial reaction to this command of peace and binding and mission from Jesus as a necessity of our daily Christian life?

How do you react when you are on the other end of community confrontation, where others are intent on holding you bound for your words, your actions, or your inactions?

Amanda Gorman, the National Youth Poet Laureate, wrote, "Cordage or Atonement," in *Call Us What We Carry:*

The future is not attained. It is atoned,
Until it is one with history,
Until home is more than memory,
Until we can hold near Who we hold dear.

What feelings and hopes do these words stir within you?

There's a story told of a teacher who gave a test to her class. When they were finished the test, the teacher told them the students would grade each other's papers. She also added that everyone would have to pass, or the class could not leave the room.

Some test results were awful, others so-so, and a few were brilliant. It was not long before an argument broke out about grades, and even just giving pass/fail grades. Why should everyone pass when some obviously didn't know the answers?

Amid the arguments, there was always someone who remembered the directions: that all had to pass or none of them would be able to leave! Finally, it was unanimous: they would all pass, though a good number of them were not happy with the outcome but didn't want to stay after school indefinitely; more were not happy because others who didn't know the right answers passed anyway.

God forgives everyone. Deep in your heart do you believe this? How do you respond when others are forgiven, and you feel like they don't "deserve it"?

Imagine this situation. You're writing a term paper and spending endless hours on it, fact-checking, adding sources, editing. But it's done. It's typed and collated and bound. You collect your project, ready to turn it in and realize reading through it that there are at least two, maybe three pages missing.

What are you going to do: spend hours looking for the lost pages, rewrite them, trying to remember, agonize over what you lost, or try to re-create them?

When Jesus first came to the rest of the disciples to proclaim he was alive and to gift them with the Spirit and send them out into the world, Thomas was missing. A week later, they were still in the locked room. Because Thomas was missing, the effect it had on all of them was devastating. His absence causes them not to go out and preach, and instead remain locked in the room in their fears. Jesus has his way of dealing with *the missing link:* tell the truth, confront the culprit, demand he reconsider, and lovingly in front of everyone, expose his ludicrous reasons for his refusal to believe the word of the others—using his own criteria, his own words, to reveal the truth of his harm to the community, his selfish choice. Is this a Jesus you are adept at imitating?

"The need today is for ethical audacity, moral guts and spiritual defiance," wrote Rabbi Abraham Joshua Heschel. Where are areas in your life you need to practice these virtues today, on your own and with others in your family, church, and community?

7

Forgiveness and the Art of Restorative Justice

Justice makes beautiful what has been deformed.

—Bonaventure

We've had enough of exhortations to be silent! Cry out with a hundred thousand tongues. I see that the world is rotten because of silence.

—Catherine of Siena

We are to give bread to those who hunger, and to those who have bread pray for and give a hunger for justice.

—Oscar Romero

Justice is the same word as *holiness* and *righteousness* used in the Hebrew Bible and in the New Testament. *Justice* is also a common name for God, and one of God's most notable attributes. Justice is what is due to every human, by their very nature as human beings. In *Pacem and Terris*, John XXIII's encyclical, the pope lists sixteen rights of justice that we all deserve: food/water; clothing/shelter; medicine/health care; education; a job/work; security; freedom from violence; hope for one's children; freedom of speech, assembly, religion, language/culture; and privacy. There is one more right of justice that many wish to add to the list: the right to immigrate. These rights of justice are what are often referred to as the corporal works of mercy, as we seek to respect and support these rights for others.

In the Hebrew Bible, *justice* is right relationship to God, to others (our neighbors), and to the earth; our shared resources; and our possessions. Justice is one of the four cardinal virtues, along with prudence, fortitude, and temperance. And in US law, it is defined as "equal access under the existing laws to basic necessities such as food, shelter, education, health care, jobs, etc." And perhaps one of the best understandings of justice is "love expressed in terms of sheer human need."

Before we look at what restorative justice entails and how it is to be practiced and shared, we need to begin with justice and understand what it means. In many cultures an old story is told that speaks about justice and where to find it. It is called the Cottage of Candles. This is how I have heard it told. Once upon a time, there was a man who sought justice with all his strength. He began by studying everything he could find about justice, in law and philosophy, in the writings of the religious leaders, and in many countries.

He had a rational sense of what justice entailed but couldn't really say he knew what justice was beyond concepts. Then he traveled far and wide, sat in on court proceedings and trials, listened to judges as they ruled in cases and decreed punishments and requirements that were necessary to make sure that justice was served. But still he felt he was missing something essential, even crucial.

And he kept traveling, asking others what justice meant to them and what it was they were seeking in their own experiences and troubles, trying to get a sense of what justice really meant for peoples' lives. And time moved on as he grew older, and still he searched for a truthful answer to the question "What is justice?"

One day he was setting out for another town and took a shortcut through another man's land that was dense with trees. As nightfall approached, he came upon a clearing. Right before him, in the center of the open space was a small cottage that was filled with light. Thinking it would be a good place to stay overnight, he went up and knocked on the door. To his surprise the door, which was unlocked, opened, and he entered. He was struck by the power of the light inside. As his eyes grew accustomed to the light, he realized the room functioned as some sort of storage. Every wall of each room was lined with rows and rows of shelves filled with candles. Each candle, mostly with small wicks were floating in oil in every sort of receptacle. Some vessels were tin, flimsy, and small; others of all sizes were made of clay, and some were even precious metals. He wandered to the next room and then the next—and realized the cottage was much larger than he had thought. The rooms seemed unending and the number of candles endless.

After wandering a bit, he saw an elderly man and woman making their way up and down the shelves, checking on all the candles. He coughed, getting their attention. They turned to him and he asked them, "What is this place? What are all these candles?"

One of them answered saying, "this is the house of life and death. These are soul candles. They represent all the people living and dying in the world today. Each candle is one person's life as they are burning out." "Like yours," they said, as they gestured toward one shelf and a row of candles. As he looked around, he realized some candles were long and tapered, some fat, some just stubs, some strong and bright, others wavering and some flickering close to extinguishing in the oil that contained them.

"Can I see mine?" he asked. He was led deeper into the cottage and they showed him a candle, rather small in a row of tins filled with oil, some containing very little oil left. The wick was smoking and bent to one side.

"This one is yours, the candle of your soul," one of them said. When he looked up again the two were gone. He looked for them but they were nowhere to be found.

He looked again, in awe that all these candles represented individuals' lives, thriving, stuttering and fading, going out as he watched. He stood before the shelf the two had indicated held his own candle. There were several others, almost identical near his own. And there was one gorgeous tall one next to them. If that was his candle–how much time did he have left?

He looked at both and was sure, looking back at his life, that he most certainly wasn't the larger one–more likely he was the one nearby. And he was fearful and distressed. He looked around for the two who had been with him just minutes before, but checking out other rooms, he didn't find either of them. As he looked, another candle on the shelf sputtered and went out. He shivered, someone had just died.

He stood once again in front of his candle and made his decision. He lifted the holder that held the larger candle and carefully poured some of the thick deep oil from the larger one into his own that had much less. He stepped back and breathed a sigh of relief. And then reached again to make sure his candle was upright and rooted in its oil. But suddenly there was an arm next to his and a hand grasping his wrist tightly. It was one of the two he had seen earlier. They looked at him and he withered under their gaze. "What have you done?" one asked.

He did not answer. And one of them spoke saying, "You wanted to know what justice was, didn't you? Is this the kind of justice you were seeking? Well now you know. In what you have done you have committed injustice and torn justice from another."

In that moment everything disappeared. The cottage

was gone, the two strangers gone, there was nothing else there in the empty clearing. He stood alone in the dark listening to the sounds of a great stillness and whispers of the night.

And he now wondered, was that his candle? What had he done? Did he know what justice was now, having taken something of life from another? As he considered this, the wind picked up and moaned around him.

It's a startling story, again leaving us with questions of how to answer the question and reflect upon our own lives—as well as consider our own sense of what justice is—or what creates injustice. Perhaps more than anything, it forces home the idea that justice isn't just about us. Justice is what binds all of us together as one. Justice tells us we are intimately and deeply connected to everyone else.

Among Jesus's parables is one that speaks of justice. It appears after Jesus's exchange with Peter, after he asks how many times he has to forgive another, seven times seven or seven times seventy-seven. You'll recall Jesus's answer, essentially saying, stop counting and start forgiving. But after that, Jesus continues with this parable.

> That is why the kingdom of heaven may be likened to a king who decided to settle accounts with his servants. When he began the accounting, a debtor was brought before him who owed him a huge amount. Since he had no way of paying it back, his master ordered him to be sold, along with his wife, his children, and his property, in payment of the debt.

> At that, the servant fell down, did him homage, and said, "Be patient with me, and I will pay you back in full." Moved with compassion, the master of that servant let him go and forgave him the loan. When the servant left, he found one of his fellow servants who owed him a much smaller amount. He seized him and started to choke him, demanding, "Pay back what you owe." Falling to his knees, his fellow servant begged him, "Be patient with me and I will pay you back." But he refused. Instead, he had him put in prison until he paid back the debt. Now when his fellow servants saw what had happened, they were deeply disturbed, and went to their master and reported the whole affair. His master summoned him and said to him: "You wicked servant! I forgave you your entire debt because you begged me to. Should you not have had pity on your fellow servant, as I had pity on you?" Then in anger his master handed him over to the torturers until he should pay back the whole debt. So will my heavenly Father do to you, unless each of you forgives his brother from your heart. (Matthew 18:23–35)

The parable is blunt and unrelenting. It echoes the phrase that we say in the Our Father: forgive us our debts as we forgive those who are in debt to us.

In the parable, there are some notable details. First is the sheer pity of the master who forgives the entire debt and sets the man free. Then there is the insensitivity and callousness of the man who after being treated so kindly then demands retribution so utterly out of proportion from what his fellow servant owes, after being caught in the same predicament.

And then read how this response "deeply disturbs" the community of the other servants. That phrase "deeply disturbs" is used rarely in the scriptures, denoting a depth of feeling that is anger, indignation, an awareness of an appalling event—and even horror. It's a word used to describe Herod's actions, when he decides to slaughter the children. And it's also the word used to describe Jesus's emotion when he prays in the garden facing what lies ahead of him with his torture and death.

In the parable, the master acts justly—treating the man he had treated with such pity who now treated another with appalling response. The king now meted out an equal sentence of strict justice for what the man did to his fellow servant.

The parable itself is disturbing, especially as we hear the last line. It declares simply that God our Father will be as just to us as we are to one another. And like the other servants, we are expected to be deeply disturbed at the injustice of those we live, work, and worship with. And together, we are to decide to right what is wrong and seek to undo the harm that others in our community do. We are to learn to abhor injustice with as much depth and response as God abhors the evil we perpetrate on one another.

This is justice.

But there is also *restorative justice.* Restorative justice is not about punishment or retribution but about healing and making whole again. Traditionally, in the Western understanding of justice, people have been concerned primarily with exacting punishment, an adversarial, top-down response meant to teach offenders a lesson and deter continued behaviors. This has been and is still practiced with little or no compensation, little or no regard for the victims of injustice and their rights.

But restorative justice holds regard for victims and their rights. Some use the image of a circle to reflect this kind of justice, where there is no beginning or end, where all are equal and all look to the center, preserving unity and community.

This is how it is described in the Navajo (Diné) justice system by Chief Justice Robert Yazzie.

> The Navajo word for "law" is *beehaz'aanii.* It means something fundamental and absolute, something that has existed from the beginning of time. Navajos believe that the Holy People "put it there for us." It's the source of a healthy, meaningful life. Navajos say that "life comes from *beehaz'aanii,*" because it is the essence of life. The precepts of *beehaz'aanii* are stated in prayers and ceremonies that tell us of "*hozhooji*"—the "perfect state." . . .
>
> Think of a system with an end goal of restorative justice, which uses equality and the full participation of disputants in a final decision. If we say of law that

> "life comes from it," then where there is hurt, there must be healing. To the Navajo way of thinking, justice is related to healing because many of the concepts are the same. When a Navajo becomes ill, he or she will consult a medicine man. A Navajo healer examines a patient to determine what is wrong, what caused the illness, and what ceremony matches the illness to cure it. The cure must be related to the cause of the illness, because Navajo healing works through two processes: it drives away or removes the cause of illness and it restores the person to good relations in solidarity with his or her surroundings and self. Patients consult Navajo healers to summon outside healing forces and to marshal what they have inside themselves for healing. (Robert Yazzie, "Life Comes from It: Navajo Justice Concepts," *New Mexico Law Review* 24, no. 2 (1994))

Restorative justice is horizontal, reaching out to include anyone connected to both the victims who experience harm and injustice, and those who have broken faith with others, shattered the balance and harmony within individual lives, disordered community life, harmed others and all their relatives and relations. Restorative justice is a community affair that is almost universal in practice, especially among Indigenous communities. We are all bound tightly together and to disturb or harm one, affects all the others.

In Navajo—Diné—this concept is called *hozho*, in Maori

it's *whakapapa*; in Bantu (South and Southeast Africa) it is *ubuntu*; in Tibetan for Buddhists, it is *tendrel*. Perhaps the best word to describe it in English is *solidarity*. We are all bound in a web of relationships with both responsibilities and obligations, but also with gifts and weaknesses that fill the gaps in one another and our communities.

In theological terms, we talk about conversion and making amends, amending our lives so that we live more in conformity and harmony with the Word of God and more in the community that is the Body of Christ. This is how it is described in the Diné tradition.

> To better comprehend Navajo justice we must understand distributive justice. Navajo court decisions place more importance on helping the victim than finding fault. On the other hand, compensating a victim in accordance with the victim's feelings and the perpetrator's ability to pay is more important than using a precise measure of damages to compensate for actual losses.
>
> Another unique aspect of Navajo justice is that the relatives of the one who causes injury are responsible to compensate the one hurt and the relatives of the injured party are entitled to the benefit of the compensation. Distributive justice is concerned with the well-being of everyone in the community. If I see a hungry person, it does not matter whether I am responsible for the hunger. If someone is injured, it is irrelevant that I did not hurt that relative. Everyone

> is a part of the community, and the resources of the community must be shared with all. . . . Restoration is more important than punishment. ("Healing as Justice: The Navajo Response to Crime," in *Justice as Healing: Indigenous Ways*, ed. Wanda D. McCaslin)

This is how justice is practiced and nourished in the Navajo community. There is a story told in Luke's Gospel that explores what this looks like in someone who listens to the Good News of Jesus and decides to follow him. It is the last story Jesus tells in his interaction with others, before he goes into Jerusalem to face the cross, his death, and resurrection. Here's how the gospel writer relays the events:

> [Jesus] came to Jericho and intended to pass through the town. Now, a man there named Zacchaeus, who was a chief tax collector and also a wealthy man, was seeking to see who Jesus was, but he could not see him because of the crowd, for he was short in stature. So he ran ahead and climbed a sycamore tree in order to see Jesus, who was about to pass that way. When he reached the place, Jesus looked up and said to him: "Zacchaeus, come down quickly, for today I must stay at your house." And he came down quickly and received him with great joy. When they all saw this, they began to grumble, saying, "He has gone to stay at the house of a sinner." But Zacchaeus stood there and said to the Lord: "Behold, half of my possessions,

Lord, I shall give to the poor, and if I have extorted anything from anyone I shall repay it four times over." And Jesus said to him: "Today salvation has come to this house because this man too is a descendant of Abraham. For the Son of Man has come to seek and to save what was lost." (Luke 19:1–10)

In this story we experience restorative justice. Jesus is not interested in assigning guilt (though the crowd definitely is). Jesus invites himself into Zacchaeus's house so that he can turn toward Jesus and accept Jesus's word and way of life.

We are told Zacchaeus is short of stature: not just short in height, but low in the estimation of the community because of who he is and the work he has done. As a tax collector he was scorned because in his role he extorted money from his neighbors, other Jews, to enhance his own status, making the lives of his own people more difficult, more destitute. As a tax collector, he lived in close collusion with the Roman government, which enslaved and humiliated Jews, despising them.

Zacchaeus is curious, though. He's really interested in "seeking to see" Jesus, having heard Jesus's preaching. He goes to great lengths to see him, even climbing a tree, an undignified venture, subjecting himself to ridicule and humiliation. But he does it to catch sight of Jesus.

And Jesus, in public, invites himself to Zacchaeus's house, knowing that they both will incur the wrath and anger of the crowd. They are described as "grumbling," but it's the word used in the Book of Exodus to describe the rebellious Israelites in the desert when they start to complain to Moses and want to go back to Egypt.

It's a deep-seated anger, jealousy, and even rage that is *murmuring* against them. But Zacchaeus stands his ground. And what he promises Jesus is staggering. First, he will give half of his possessions to the poor, which would have radically altered his economic status and standing in the community. But he goes further: if he has defrauded or taken anything from anyone unlawfully, he will pay them back fourfold.

Jesus is delighted when Zacchaeus jumps down out of the tree and the sinner welcomes him with joy. And again, Jesus reacts with joy to his profession of belief in Jesus and the covenant he makes with Jesus about the future of his life. The future he promises is pure restorative justice toward everyone in his family, the religious community, and his fellow Jews.

The promises of restoration also happen to be the requirements for baptism in Luke's community. When they submitted to Jesus's Word of Good News to the Poor, they did the same: half of everything to the poor and fourfold justice: in baptism restorative justice was a Christian beginning to follow Jesus's way of living. And it wasn't just done once as part of the baptismal ritual; it was reenacted every year during Lent when the new believers were initiated into the community, by the *older* Christians—a time of recommitment to their baptism and the way of restorative justice: the way of Jesus.

This is basic and foundational to living as a Christian. Individuals need to live restorative justice as intrinsic to their personal spirituality. And also, there must be a commitment that communities, churches, and nations must learn of restorative justice as core to living in society. God's vision for all nations is this biblical sense of restorative justice that reaffirms a human community that respects, honors, and celebrates cultural and ethnic diversity. Our emphasis on individual spirituality has often ignored what this looks like in relation to others and to society, the family of nations worldwide. And one way this commitment is described comes from the American bishops in their pastoral letter on the Fifth Centenary ("The Drama of Evangelization," in *Heritage and Hope,* United States Catholic Conference, 1991):

> The encounter with the Europeans was a harsh and painful one for the Indigenous peoples. The unwitting introduction of diseases to which the Native Americans had no immunities led to the deaths of millions. Added to that were the cultural oppression, the injustices, the disrespect for native ways and traditions that must be acknowledged and lamented. The first great wave of European colonization was accompanied by a destruction of Native American civilization, the violent usurpation of their lands, and the brutalization of the inhabitants. Many of those associated with the conquest of the new lands failed

to see in the natives the workings of the same God that they espoused.

God's dream of reconciliation and peace is built on restorative justice. Jesus's compassionate identification with the least, the outcast and those who hunger for justice, based on forgiveness, reconciliation and restorative justice, healing, and making peace among all peoples is the foundation of all theology and spirituality.

Like Zacchaeus's covenant with God expressed in his conversion to live serving all others, all of us must personally begin to be reconverted to the gospel, the beatitudes, and Jesus's call to forgive, reconcile, and restore wholeness and holiness in our institutions, groups, churches, societies, and nations.

We are far behind in integrating restorative justice in all aspects of our lives. And we must begin again—and yet again, to restore justice as a vital force for communion and solidarity among all people.

There is a simple story-image from a midrash in the Jewish prayer book, *Adonai Eloheinu* (Our Ruler Our God) which states the reasons for the many names of God. *Adonai* always appears before the name *Eloheinu* because *Adonai* stands for God's mercy, while *Eloheinu* stands for God's justice. We must remember God's mercy first. The midrash continues with a short story. A king was given the gift of a new drinking glass and two drinks were brought to him to drink. One was a wine so hot he was afraid to pour it into his new glass thinking it might shatter as the wine coated it. But the other wine was ice cold and he was equally afraid it would crack the glass. So, he poured both wines into the glass at the same time, protecting the glass. It is said that mercy is the hot drink and justice the cold one.

When God was deciding how to create his world, he mulled over how to do it. If he created the world and constructed it only of justice, then when humans did evil or harmed each other, he would have to right the wrong and stop the harm. But if he created the world with only mercy, then humans would get away with never repenting, continuing to do evil, wreck the world and destroy one another. So, it is said, when God created the world, he decided to use equal measures of both justice and mercy. And in that way the world survives along with all its peoples (Midrash Genesis Rabbah 12:15, as told by Rossel in *When a Jew Prays*).

> *I am often struck by the dangerous narcissism fostered by spiritual rhetoric that pays so much attention to individual self-improvement and so little to the practice of love within the context of community.*
>
> —bell hooks

> *We link resurrection with liberation because our deepest need is not personal immortality but a life before death for everyone. I believe the strongest sign of the*

new life is solidarity and where there is solidarity there is resurrection.

—Dorothee Soelle

I don't believe in charity. I believe in solidarity. Charity is vertical, so it's humiliating. It goes from the top to the bottom. Solidarity is horizontal. It respects the other and learns from the other.

—Eduardo Galeano

We have to be militants for kindness, subversive for sweetness, and radicals for tenderness.

—Cornel West

INTENTION, REFLECTION, RESPONSE

An offender can be punished. But to punish and not restore—that is the greatest of all offenses. . . . [I]f a man takes unto himself God's right to punish, then he must also take upon himself God's promise to restore.

—Alan Paton, *Too Late the Phalarope*

When you think of punishing someone, do you also think of how to restore that person's dignity and your own relationship to them? Do you learn anything about yourself when you try to do both in these situations?

Do not get lost in a sea of despair. Do not become bitter or hostile. Be hopeful. Be optimistic. Never ever be afraid to make some noise and get in good trouble, necessary trouble. We will find a way to make a way out of no way.

—John Lewis, June 27, 2018

Do you have a group of people, a gang of friends or neighbors who help you when you need to get into "good trouble"? Restoration is always more powerful and more possible when practiced with others.

But let us teach solidarity, walking with the victims, serving and loving. I offer this for you to consider—downward mobility. And I would say in this enterprise there is a great deal of hope.

—Dean Brackley, S.J.

Look at the people around you, in your neighborhood, your church community, where you work, and in the city where you dwell. Who are people in need of your solidarity? Can you work with a few other people to create restorative relationships with some of these people?

In Navajo communities, small groups of people who live in proximity to one another, in clans, tribes, and geographical areas, often choose a *naat'aanii*, someone who functions as a peace maker, who takes a leadership role in drawing people together in the face of adversity, crime, suffering, and death within families and communities. They are persons, men and women, greatly respected in the community, elders or those who serve in other capacities such as education, counseling, health care. Or they may be someone who knows and listens to many in the community. They listen, counsel, ask questions, dialogue, get families to talk with one another, act as a guide and a go-between with members of neighborhoods and extended families. They help everyone to resolve difficulties, keep avenues of communication open, keep people talking to one another, and encourage those who are silent, fearful, or not usually included to be a part of the circle of those who seek to do restorative justice.

Make a list—or if you are in a group context, together make a list—and name these people who are *naat'aanii*, or *curandaras/os* (healers) or trusted people who others go to when they need help. These people would also be known for seeking out those in distress or trouble, who otherwise are not being included or served in their communities.

There is an anecdote told in Buddhist zendos that can remind us of another way to look at what's going on around us or problems we initially perceive in someone's behavior. They say, imagine to yourself that you're in a boat, kayak, or canoe, alone on a lake, and fog rolls in. You head for the shore as quickly as you can, trying not to panic. Then you become dimly aware that there is another boat somewhere near you that seems to be heading in your direction. You cry out a warning, yell for the people to identify themselves and where they are. But there is no response, and with the fog the wind comes up and they seem to be coming closer, faster.

You become even more agitated, because they seem intent on slamming into you even though you are loudly announcing where you are, trying to steer clear of them.

Then the other boat hits you hard. You yell in fear and anger, trying to push the other boat away from you so you don't capsize. Only then do you realize the boat is empty—there's no one in the other boat. It was the wind, the currents that set the other boat in your direction and caused both of you to crash into one another.

Are there situations and experiences in your life that cause you to react in anger, fear, aggressive reactions to others, even rage, and hate, when in reality these situations aren't caused by a particular individual, but rather by circumstances, as something "just happens"? When you realize that it's not someone else's fault, what is it you do with your anger, frustration, and rage?

Off the coast of Scotland is an island called Discussion Island. People were sent there to resolve their differences and make peace with one another. They were given cheese and whiskey to share while they were there, but they did not return until things were settled between them.

Do you have your own place to go to ease tensions and open conversations that lead to settling dissension? Imagine where a place like this would be—and what it would be like—for your communities.

The Navajo have a simple process to start the experience of restorative justice with others. It includes six simple steps:

1. Begin with prayer for everyone involved, appealing to the power and wisdom of the Great Spirit, the Creator, to be a part of those gathered together.

2. Then each person talks about what happened, what the problem or issue is from their point of view, along with their feelings, describing how this situation is affecting them. There are no interruptions, comments, or questions: everyone listens to each speaker with attention and respect.
3. Then the *naat'aanii*, an elder, teacher, or religious leader seeks to offer some wisdom, insight, perspective from their experience and their traditions, history, stories, and rituals. They may suggest prayers or laws related to where everyone "stands" and propose what actions and response can be taken now.
4. Again, all parties discuss where they are now: the victims, those who are opponents or perpetrators, the leaders, members of the parties' families, and those invited in as guests with expertise and background who can help the community deal with their reactions, as well as those who will eventually speak the judgments that the community decides upon. All of this takes time, patience, calmness, periods of silence, and reflection, as everyone tries to understand the reasons why something harmful happened.
5. With a goal of restorative justice, everyone tries to come to an agreement on what should be done, by the perpetrator(s), the victims, their relatives, and all the rest of the community that is involved in supporting and repairing the relationships within the group. This is the actual reconciliation process of how they will *walk together again* as individuals, in twos and threes, as families, and in small groups as well as the whole community.
6. Everyone now tries to express consensus based on all they have experienced together when they gathered

> and began with prayer. Each one tries to articulate something connected to consensus in agreement with others. It is decided what they will do, who does each particular action, and who will initiate and follow up on decisions made, as well as review how the process is developing. What is agreed upon is practical. If consensus is verbal, it must be something done that—for or with those involved—helps to heal and solidify better relations among the individuals in question. Usually, this step ends in a covenant that is put in writing and signed by everyone in the group, as witnesses to their intent and hopes for restored harmony, balance, and peace among everyone.

The agreement meets as a community where—*Mitakuye Oyasin*—the traditional Diné blessing, prayer, welcome, or acknowledgment of all groups and individuals is spoken when meeting together in rituals, prayers, or simply conversation: "All my relations" and shared as a kind of blessing of "Peace be with you."

8

After Violence, Trauma, Grief

True resistance begins with people confronting pain–and wanting to do something to change it.

–bell hooks

What hurts the victim most is not the cruelty of the oppressor but the silence of the bystander.

–Elie Wiesel

Violence–in all its vicious forms we have experienced and that have been inflicted upon us–is one of the hardest realities we have to live with, to forgive, and to somehow absorb. We do this by restoring our balance, equilibrium, and ability to live and to love again.

Violence breaks our hearts, tears at our souls, shreds our dignity and self-worth, poisons our minds, leaves its marks on our flesh, and overwhelms our relationships.

It murders so much within us. More than any other kind of pain, violence confronts us with our vulnerability, our humanity, and who we are as the beloved children of God.

Reactions to violence and the enduring pain it inflicts upon us gives us the experience of Job in the Bible: beset by an endless stream of disasters, coming from every side, in all areas of life. In the book of Job, he speaks constantly of what he is trying to bear. "I will speak in the anguish of my spirit; I will complain in the bitterness of my soul" (Job 7:8).

When we meet with violence, often our initial reaction is to blame God for the evil that happens. "Why have you set me up as an object of attack: or why should I be a target for you? . . . I waste away: I cannot live forever; let me alone, for my days are but a breath" (Job 7:12, 16). We question God vehemently. Pain invades us and takes over every moment of our lives. Whether it is the death of a child, or a random attack on a group of people, a suicide, or a massacre of children, violence sets in motion cycles of suffering that we do not know how to endure or cope with, individually or within our communities.

Violence attacks a person, violating their sacredness, whether it is physical, psychological, emotional, or spiritual. Violence is personal, individual, enacted against groups, those of other genders, religions, races, nations—or even random and anonymous.

We must somehow begin a process of undoing the dishonor that has been done and reclaim our sacredness. To do this, we must first begin with our grief, sadness, tears, or our acknowledgment that we are perhaps numb, not able to mourn and weep.

Grief is the last act of love we must give to those we loved. Where there is deep grief, there was great love. All of us know illness, the death of others we love, slow, disease-ridden, unexpected, accidental, violent, or peaceful. It always does violence to our hearts, our souls and spirits in varying degrees depending on how it happens.

Let us begin with a story of death, loss, the violence of hunger that kills the young, the aging, and the weak. It is an old First Nations' story from the area called Bitter Root in Montana, near the Canadian border. Once upon a time, there came a harsh winter that seemed to go on forever. The people grew short on what they had stored over the summer and autumn months and were reduced to trying to dig roots and chew on whatever might have some nutrients in what they foraged.

The hunters went out daily, but game was scarce, and they grew weak from lack of food. It was the very young ones, the elderly, and sick that starting dying first. Then the young mothers, the pregnant ones. And still it snowed.

Finally, a grandmother couldn't bear watching her grandchildren die any longer. She shared whatever she could find with them, but it wasn't near enough. And so, she decided it was time for her to die. There would be one less adult mouth to feed, a small bit for the others who needed it more. She went out early one freezing morning, down by the river still frozen solid where it was her custom to pray to the Great Spirit. She knelt in the snow and sang, wailing softly, telling the Great Spirit of the suffering of her family, her tribe, and all the people. How much they had tried to keep one another alive, yet there was never enough. So, she would lay down her life, let go of all she loved so dearly so that others might have life a bit longer. As she sang, a bird started singing on a branch just above her.

She looked up and caught sight of it in the barren branches. It was bright scarlet, like blood, red against the snow and sky. It sang back to her and she realized that it was telling her to look around her at the ground she was kneeling on. As she looked closely she noticed tiny plants sticking out of the snow. They were white too, a tinge or two of green leaves underneath the petals. She'd never seen anything like this plant and flower before. She sensed she should take her digging stick, tied to her belt, and dig some of them up. She did, carefully collecting them, putting them in her cloth bag.

And the bird sang, telling her that she was to go home and boil the leaves making a tea of them, and use the stem and the flowers to chew on, and then share them with her people. It was a gift from the Great Spirit for her people in response to her prayer and the offering of her life.

She offered her thanks and went back to the village, making the tea and sharing the plant. It was bitter, sharp, but it tasted too of freshness that was green and it helped them through the last days of the snow before it melted.

The plant was called Bitter Root and it appears only late in February and March when the snow is slow to melt and it is hard to find food. Even the valley and the fork of the river where it grows is named Bitter Root in thanksgiving for the gift that was given when the people knew hunger, the ache and pain of heartache, and the dying of children, the elderly, and the weak, as the others sought to survive.

During winter, the story is told to remind the people that gifts are given in times of great need, death, and suffering. New life always follows on such hardship, grief, and loss.

We return to this process of restoration and healing by remembering and telling the stories of violence inflicted, borne, and taken into our bodies and souls. Elie Wiesel, who wrote stories of the Holocaust, of massive death and destruction, in his own family, religious community of Jews, and nation also wrote stories as a link between the awful experiences of violence and in spite of everything, the ability and power to not only live again but defy violence and despair to convert even death into hope, rejoicing, and life.

Often, he began his stories with these words: "You want a description of the indescribable? There is no way to describe the indescribable. But let me tell you a story."

In the Gospel of Matthew there is one such indescribable pain told in a story that draws us back into the memory of murder, innocent death, shared pain and the madness and insanity of violence. The story is told as the *ending* of the Christmas account. After Jesus is born in Bethlehem, we hear the ancient stories and songs of magi, astrologers from the East coming into Jerusalem. They have followed a star that signaled the birth of the newborn king of the Jews. When they first arrive in the region, they go to Herod, a notorious king, evil to the bone, whose history included killing his relatives, wives, and even his own children in fear of competition to his throne and rule. When the magi—the wise men—tell Herod of the child's birth, he and the whole city are *deeply disturbed*— a phrase used in scriptures to warn of impending death and violence. Political power is deeply disturbed by new life and the hope of liberation and freedom breaking into the established order.

Herod acts shrewdly, getting all the information he can from the scribes and priests about the prophecies of the Messiah to be born in Bethlehem. Then he elicits information about the background of the men who followed the star from the exact time of the star's appearance. He discerns from the information, the general age of the child. And when he sends the magi off to Bethlehem, he gets them to agree to return to him with more specific information, so that in his words he can go and "offer him homage too."

When the magi leave his presence, his palace, the star again appears and goes ahead of them to the place where they find the child with his parents. Arriving, they "prostrate themselves and do him homage." They then empty their coffers and give the child their gifts.

But then they receive "a message in a dream not to return to Herod, so they went back to their own country by another route" (Matthew 2:12). And their story in the gospel ends. They never appear again. That saying among storytellers rings true here: "The story begins when the teller stops talking."

The magi go home empty-handed to their new life having met and encountered the child, Jesus. But they disobey Herod and do not return to give him any information. This infuriates Herod, driving him to react viciously.

With the information he's gathered from the scribes, priests, and the magi, Herod moves to destroy any possibility that there is a child who might grow up to take his throne. Matthew's account continues:

> Once Herod realized he had been deceived by the astrologers, he became furious. He ordered the massacre of all the boys two years old and under in Bethlehem and its environs, making his calculations on the basis of the date he had learned from the astrologers. What was said though Jeremiah the prophet was then fulfilled:
>
> A cry was heard at Ramah, sobbing and loud lamentation: Rachel bewailing her children; no comfort for her, since they are no more. (Matthew 2:16–18)

In those few lines the violence of Christmas reaches its conclusion. We learn in the previous lines that Joseph too has had a dream. In the dream he is commanded to "Get up, take the child and his mother, and flee to Egypt. Stay there until I tell you otherwise. Herod is searching for the child to destroy him" (Matthew 2:12). Joseph obeys.

But the violence has been set in motion. One child lives with the parents' memories of the slaughter of all the others caught up in a militaristic operation, forced immigration, the making of a family into refugees, and long exile in a foreign country. And many families experience the death of their children, the destruction of their families, and the reality of the fragility of life under oppression, poverty, and misery. The words of Jeremiah echo into this moment of the one who has become a mother: "Rachel refuses to be consoled."

The story is shattering, filled with horror, despair, and loss. How do we impose meaning on such violence? Wiesel and similar writers are adamantly clear: if we do not speak out against such pain and suffering, it is inexcusable—we not only add to those who suffer but are responsible in part for the effects of such violence.

We only need to look at our own contemporary histories to find this violence in endless experiences: wars, occupations, genocides, random mass killings, school shootings, police violence against young Black men like George Floyd, one group hating another and seeking to exterminate their *enemies* whom they see as different from them, old hatreds festering and erupting from one generation to the next, one nation seeing another as a threat—even singling out the children in violence, the innocent slaughtered over time, impoverished, abused, in forced labor, slow starvation, humiliated, shamed and removed from their families, their land, and their traditions.

How do we undo the harm done in such situations and relationships? How do we and our communities—who have experienced and reexperienced trauma and abuse over generations—respond?

In remembrance. *Remembering* is the first step in any healing, restoring of life and possibilities, forgiving and creating life out of the chaos, violation, and desecration. That's what many people have learned from their own histories and stories. And this is the way a Jewish rabbi, Harold Kushner, in his book *When Bad Things Happen to Good People,* speaks of remembering.

> Only human beings can defeat death by summoning the memory of someone they loved and lost, and feeling that person close to them as they do so. . . . Memory can be painful, as everything that makes a human being more than an animal can be painful. Good memories deepen the poignancy of what we have lost. Bad memories keep the resentment alive when the occasion is long past. But memory is what ultimately gives us power over death; by keeping the person alive in our hearts. Memory is what gives us power over time by keeping the past present so it cannot fade and rob us of what we once held precious—we have all the yesterdays we are capable of remembering and all the tomorrows we can envision.

Once when I was listening to a Native woman tell her long story of grief, loss, and how it had become a burden that she dragged around with her always, as it invaded her prayer, her relationships with her husband, her children and entire family, she said (through cracked words and tears) that "people keep telling me to 'move on,' 'get over it,' 'leave it behind me.' They don't realize I can't. I'm trying to carry it gently, tend to it and bring it with me as I continue to live."

As we talked, I shared with her what I had heard Joy Harjo, a First Nations' poet, writer, and musician, tell a group of women sharing their grief. Quoting a poem she wrote in 2015, "For Calling the Spirit Back from Wandering the Earth in Its Human Feet," she said, "Call your spirit back. It may be caught in corners and creases of shame; judgment and human abuse. / You must call in a way that your spirit will want to return. / Speak to it as you would a beloved child." It is where we begin, and begin again, and again in a new way of being and living with loss.

This kind of trauma, loss, and pain is something Jesus himself experienced, living in Israel, under the brutal regime of the Herods and those who ruled after their deaths. Israel was an occupied military territory, with far more slaves than free, with massive poverty, human misery, starvation, and oppression. And Jesus himself knew the violence of hate, plots, and intent to kill him that were politically, economically, and religiously based. That violence of hate would in the future bring him to physical torture, public humiliation, shame, and brutal execution used to teach others fear and submission. And it would be fueled and abetted by not only political leaders but religious leaders who sought to end his teaching of solidarity with the poorest of the earth.

We read of Jesus's response, when it's clear what they are doing to him, and their intention to kill him. Luke's Gospel brings us to the scene:

> Coming within sight of the city, [Jesus] wept over it and said: "If only you had known the path to peace this day; but you have completely lost it from view. Days will come upon you when your enemies encircle you with a rampart, hem you in, and press you hard from every side. They will wipe you out, you and your children within your walls, and leave not a stone on a stone within you, because you failed to recognize the time of your visitation." (Luke 19:41–44)

Jesus wept. We know from other stories in the gospels that he wept over the death of his friend Lazarus, and he wept over an entire city that knew persecution, slavery, war, human misery, and poverty. His message, his life, all he sought to do, was to bring peace to the souls and personal lives of all the people. He sought to teach people to live in peace with one another, to forgive, reconcile, do justice, and restore fullness of life to those most in need, the least of people in his society and world.

Jesus, visited earth in the Incarnation, our God-Father becoming our flesh and dwelling with us, being peace among us. And as he nears the end of his life, overlooking the city and the people he loved and sought to serve, he wept. He wept for all the pain they had known, knew, and would know in the future. In our suffering our God weeps over us, over our pain and loss. In Jesus, he carried a depth of grief that includes all that we mourn and bear in our lives.

So, we do not bear our grief or mourn alone. There is a Muslim story told called Jesus's Patchwork Cloak of Wool. It is said that Jesus, son of Mary, had a patchwork cloak, and he even wore it when he ascended into heaven! It is said that many have seen him in dreams wearing that cloak patched, torn, ragged and worn woolen, frayed and in tatters. But at the same time, many have said that same cloak had rays and beams of light shining from every inch. Those who have seen him wearing that cloak also have recounted how Jesus told them: "These are the rays of my misery. Every rip and tear which I had to mend, all the pangs and stabs of suffering of others which stung my heart and tore it to shreds. I bear them still and continue my work of turning your pain to light." Once, when I once told this story, an elder told me, "Yes, when he looks at us, when we suffer, he adds it to his cloak as he wraps his cloak and his arms around us." Now every time I tell this story, I must add her words. That's how the story continues.

We begin with memory, remembering our sorrows, and the violence we have known in our flesh and soul. Then we tell our pains aloud, sharing them with others. There is a very short fable from Aesop. A girl was stung by sharp nettles as she walked through a field. She immediately ran home in tears, crying to her mother. I only brushed by them, she said, touching them gently, trying to be careful, but it hurts so bad. And it doesn't stop. Surprisingly, her mother told her, "That's why it stung you. The next time you touch a nettle, grasp it tightly, and it will not hurt so much." Somehow, we must seize hold of our pain and by facing it—squeezing it tightly—take some of the sting out of it.

We must share our pain and make others aware of our suffering. The theologian Gregory Baum once said, "To be wounded by the suffering of others is a gift of the Holy Spirit." We must be heard and others must hear, listen, and share our pain.

To not listen, to not make ourselves available to others, or to refuse to listen is not merely insensitivity, but evil on our part. Elie Wiesel painfully reminds us that "What hurts the victim the most is not the cruelty of the oppressor but the silence of the bystander." We are not allowed to ignore the pain of others, especially all that results from violence, abuse, humiliation, and shaming. Healing from violence cannot be done alone. If, as Thomas Merton said, "Love is our true destiny, then we do not find the meaning of life by ourselves alone . . . we find it with others." The first essential and crucial steps in healing, in forgiveness, and in reconciliation are done with others.

One story I have heard came to me from different contexts, told by someone in the Hindu tradition and again by an old Navajo man after a healing ceremony.

Once upon a time, an old teacher got tired of one of his young students constantly complaining–about the weather, the food, others, and what he was feeling. It was a never-ending litany. Finally, one afternoon, he sent him on an errand. Go and get me some salt. He returned with a handful of salt and was told to put it into a cup of water and then drink it. Reluctantly he obeyed and was asked, "How does it taste?" "Awful! Bitter!" the student answered as he choked and spit it out.

Then the teacher told him and a few of the others, "Let's go for a walk and each of you take a handful of salt with you." They went down by a lake. When they got to the lake's edge, he told them, "All of you, throw the salt into the lake." They did. "Now, drink." It had been a hot day, and they drank and drank, cupping the water in their hands, even just lapping it up bent over the water. *Hmmm.*

He then said, "What's it taste like now?" They were enthusiastic: fresh, clear, biting cold. "Any salt?" he asked.

"None!" they responded.

So, he told them, "The pain in your life, and there is and will be a lot of it, is pure salt. You will have to deal with that amount of 'salt' as you know pain and suffering, violence, loss, and grieving. But the amount of bitterness and what you bear and carry with you over time depends on the container you put it in. It's your soul, your spirit, your heart. How large is it? How deep is it? How strong is it? All you can do in life, is enlarge your heart, deepen your soul, stretch your spirit so that you can bear it all.

Don't be a glass, or a pitcher, or gourd—be a lake, be a freshwater river."

Remembering, grieving, mourning, and tears are the ways we begin to absorb and transform violence, trauma, physical and mental anguish, emotional, psychological, and even religious pain. The Jewish midrash that offers wisdom stories linked to theology tells one of the origin of tears. It begins with God speaking to Adam and Eve when they find themselves outside the garden. "My dearest children, I am so sorry that you are suffering and that now you will live and learn the lessons of earth, time, and growth. You are already beginning to know what it means to endure, and to experience loss and pain, but I want you to know that I will always be with you and that my love for you is never ending.

"To make it a little easier, and comfort you, I am giving you a gift to help you through the hard times, the pain and suffering that is a part of living and dying. The gift looks like a pearl, a soft, wet pearl. It comes from your heart, through your eyes. It wells up and falls down your face. Whenever you feel like your heart is about to break, you will feel my gift filling up your eyes, overflowing and sliding down your face. It is called a 'tear.' It is a drop of water formed from within your soul and my Spirit and when you feel it you will sense something changing and shifting inside you. It can make you feel lighter, freer, less lonely, less overwhelmed with sorrow.

"You will always have as many tears as you need throughout your whole life. To be able to weep, to cry and shed your tears will be a gift to help you breathe more deeply and know you are still alive and loved deeply. Your tears can ease the aches deep with you, and open you to living and loving again.

"There will be other gifts that will help you to weep and share your tears: places you love, memories, a piece of clothing, song, dance and drum, music, silence, being out in nature, animals, birds, trees to lean up against, the ocean, standing under the starlight and deep darkness, friends who just stay present with you, listen, hold you, and always I will be with you."

Among Jesus's blessings, his beatitudes, we find the words "Blessed are you who mourn, for you shall be comforted" (Matthew 5:4). We are made in God's image. Tears are prayers, too. They travel to God when we have no voice and cannot speak.

Tears are also a part of a wider healing vision that in Jewish spirituality is called *tikkun olam:* repairing the world—something we'll look at more in the following chapters. As we grieve, we ask our deepest questions: "How do we repair our souls, repair our relationships, and repair structures and institutions that are rent and torn by violence. How do we restore and re-create life, 'ever more abundantly' after trauma, violence and loss?"

Repair is the next step in the process of forgiving, reconciling, restoring justice. We repair our bodies and souls to live in the freedom of the beloved children of our God, Maker and Keeper, Giver of Life.

No daylight to separate us. Only kinship. Inching ourselves closer to creating a community of kinship such that God might recognize it. Soon we imagine, with God, this circle of compassion. Then we imagine no one standing outside of that circle, moving ourselves closer to the margins so that the margins themselves will be erased.

—Gregory Boyle, SJ

The darker the night, the brighter the stars. The deeper the grief, the closer is God!

—Fyodor Dostoevsky

INTENTION, REFLECTION, RESPONSE

We hear in the story of Joseph, Mary. and Jesus's escape into Egypt, running from King Herod's soldiers and the killing of the children. And we hear of Rachel, weeping for her children, "sobbing with loud lamentation, bewailing, with no comfort, for they are no more." Rachel, one of Jacob's wives, was his most beloved. For many years she lives a story of barrenness, but at long last has two children, Joseph and then Benjamin. She dies giving birth to her youngest boy. And she is buried by the side of the road. One of the Mothers of Israel, she looks out for all her children (newly born and growing old) dispersed over the whole world. In the book of Genesis, she is portrayed as caring for all her people, begging God for mercy on them. She is also recognized as the one who by her prayers convinced God to return Israelites home from exile.

The prophet Jeremiah records God's words to her and all her lost children: "Cease your cries of mourning, wipe the tears from your eyes. The sorrow you have shown shall have its reward, says the Lord, they shall return from the enemies' land. There is hope for your future, says the Lord: Your sons shall return to their own borders" (Jeremiah 31:15–17).

Even today, Rachel's tomb is a place of pilgrimage and prayer, a place where those who mourn those they've lost come to weep, to scream in interior pain and outward silence, and to pray for those they love.

Do you have, can you find or create places you can go, alone and with others, to pray, to hold silent vigil, to weep? Or when you can't cry, a place to bring your mourning for those you have lost? Think of Miriam (Mary), Jesus's mother, praying with the relatives of the children murdered in Bethlehem, while they escaped? Hold the memory of pain with Rachel, with Miriam (whose name means sea of bitterness and sorrow), with those who love all you yourself have lost. Your prayers rise and are heard. Our God in Jesus came to change our violent world to one of peace, restored life, and resurrection.

You think your pain and heartbreak are unprecedented in the history of the world but then you read. It was books that taught me that the things that tormented me the most were the very things that connected me with all the people who were alive, who had ever been alive." (James Baldwin, "Telling Talk from a Negro Writer.")

Make a short list of writers and their books that have touched you, moved you to tears, been witness to their sorrows. Read them to yourself, taking heart from others' sorrow and loss. Better still, read these books with others, sharing your community's wisdom and insight to feed your mind, heart, and soul as you mourn.

Here's a list I created that you might find helpful: Wilma Mankiller, Leslie Marmon Silko, Joy Harjo, Simone Weil, Rebecca Solnit, Barry Lopez, Barbara Kingsolver, Oscar Romero, James Baldwin, Amanda Gorman, Dorothy Day, Dan Berrigan, Thomas Merton, Bell Hooks, Wendell Berry, and Pedro Casaldáliga. There are many to read, from the past and those still writing among us.

Among the books in the Hebrew Bible is the book of Lamentations, a book of prayers, reflections, cries, and laments that express pain, grief, and suffering over destruction, murder, humiliation, death, and despair. Woven in and through the lament is faith and an unquenchable hope in God's love. The words of the book seek to repair the shattered lives of individuals and of peoples bruised and broken by their experiences. Some say the book was written in the voice of a desolate widow with words meant to be chanted and sung by a person leading others in communal longing. The longing is expressed in one voice within a community, seeking compassion from God that those in pain might share with one another. The book is only five short chapters. You can dip into the book and echo some of those words to express your own mourning—especially when the tears won't rise and you are bereft and empty. Words like this touch us deeply and move us to pray and even to heal:

> Come, all you who pass by the way, look and see whether there is any suffering like my suffering, which has been dealt me. . . . At this I weep, my eyes run with tears: far from me are all who could console me, any who might revive me; my sons were reduced to silence when the enemy prevailed. (Lamentations 1:12, 16)

As you read, you may wish to keep in mind that the people whose pain is expressed in the book, collected their pain and cried out to God, aware that their suffering was in part put upon them, like Rachel, at the loss of her children, and partly the result of their own infidelity and failure to obey God.

Chapter 3 is written from the point of view of the prophet praying and speaking on behalf of all the people. He speaks not against God but against their *enemies*—all those oppressing them, harming them, killing and causing them distress. It is not God who causes violence but human beings. And our lamentations reflect the pain of oppression as well as the prayer directed toward God to intervene on our behalf and restore us, giving us new life in the midst of all that has befallen us.

> *Forgiving is the only reaction which does not merely re-act but acts anew and unexpectedly, unconditioned by the act which provoked it and therefore freeing from its consequences both the one who forgives and the one who is forgiven.*
>
> —Hannah Arendt, *The Human Condition*

Somehow even after we have known violence, trauma, and death dealt out to us, or we have been caught in its consequences, we are called to forgive and not let the experience further destroy us. One of the first steps in recovering from the violence, a step to stop the effects of experience from further harming us, is to try to imagine forgiving the one or ones causing harm.

Sister Dianna Ortiz, a Roman Catholic missionary working as a grade school teacher in Guatamala in 1989, was abducted, raped, and tortured for twenty-four hours before being released. A spokesperson for other victims of torture and a teacher of peace until her death in 2021, she wrote:

> *At the core of the human spirit, there is a voice that is stronger than violence and fear.*

9

Tikkun Olam: Repairing Our Souls

Everything is held together by stories. That is all that is holding us together: stories and compassion.

—Barry Lopez

I love myself when I am laughing . . . and then again when I'm looking mean and impressive.

—Zora Neale Hurston

There has been a wisdom teaching since early in Judaism called *tikkun olam*, from the Hebrew meaning to repair the world. It is considered by many spiritual writers to be the basis of all meaning and practice in Jewish life. It is a concept intimately connected to Jesus's words of being and bringing "life ever more abundantly" into the world (John 10). The story describing the roots of *tikkun olam* come from the fourteenth-century wisdom tradition, and one of the earliest versions of this creation story is found in Mishnah Avot 2:21.

Once upon a time, before time, in the beginnings of the world, the world was whole. But somehow there was an accident and the world was shattered, scattering all its pieces into sparks of wholeness through all creation. The sparks landed everywhere, in people, places, animals, birds, sea creatures in water, air, fire, wood, earth, into everything that exists.

But it is told that the human race, all human beings, is a response to that accident. We were born so that we can discover and uncover the hidden sparks of wholeness that hide or are buried in everything. They're in people, groups, organizations, elements, nations, all things like arts, science, all forms of knowledge, even events.

We were created to find the sparks, grasp hold of them, lift them up, expose them, make them stronger, and show them to others. We were born to restore and re-create the world, to repair its brokenness and make it whole, healing it and making it as it was originally meant to be and become.

This work has been called the birthright of all human beings. We were created by the Holy One to repair the world with him, continuing creation, gathering all the sparks back together again. This was and is the divine intent of creation from the beginning. This is the underlying mystery found in creation and in our lives.

Rabbi Tirzah Firestone in her book *Wounds into Wisdom: Healing Intergenerational Jewish Trauma*, tells it this way.

In the beginning of time, God was everywhere. But God was lonely, and wanted to be known. So, God decided to bring the world into being. To make room for creation, God drew in a first breath to make an empty space in which the world might come into being. Into this empty space, God emanated a brilliant white light. And vessels came into being in which this divine light could be held and contained.

The light flowed continuously like a luminous river, filling every space it could find. The vessels filled up, but then they began to quake. They could barely contain the voluminous stream of dazzling light. Rumbling fiercely, the vessels flew apart, shattering into millions of pieces, sending sparks of the white light like seeds and stars far and wide.

Each spark came to be encased in one of the millions of broken shards, which buried its sparkling light deep within. To this day, we are still finding and uncovering the hard casings around the sparks of the world, freeing their light so that they can shine again.

We were born to make the world, all creation, and all people in the universe whole, healing and repairing all that was from the beginnings of the world. Each of us, all of us, have these sparks of light within us, and it is our privilege and our power to set them free.

After our experiences of violence, suffering, trauma and being broken and battered, we can begin the work of healing, repairing, and restoring our souls. *Tikkun olam* shows us how, as does the teaching of Jesus.

A few stories in the gospels tell us how Jesus repairs individuals' lives, sometimes mangled and shattered in the past, still barely surviving from the effects of the violence and trauma they experienced. This is one of Jesus's stories of restoring and repairing of a woman who had been bent, doubled-over, and suffering for eighteen years.

> On a Sabbath day he was teaching in one of the synagogues. There was a woman there who for eighteen years had been possessed by a spirit which drained her strength. She was badly stooped—quite incapable of standing erect. When Jesus saw her, he called her to him and said: "Woman, you are free of your infirmity." He laid his hand on her, and immediately she stood up straight and began thanking God. (Luke 13:10–14)

On a Sabbath day—and in a synagogue—Jesus healed the woman. At the time of Jesus, synagogues were usually three-sided buildings with the back open to the street. The *bimah*, where the scrolls of the Torah were kept in an ark in the front of the synagogue, was where the teacher or leader stood to speak and lead the community in prayer. The women would have been on one side and the men on the other with a narrow space between them. Jesus would have been standing in the front, next to the Torah scrolls as he taught the congregation. The woman was most probably in the very back of the women's section, on the fringe of the community, perhaps even standing half under the overhang and half in the street.

First, Jesus sees her. She'd been coming to the synagogue for eighteen years, and likely no one ever noticed her or spoke with her. Eighteen years living on the edge of all areas of her life. She is described as "possessed by a spirit which drained her strength." We tend to think immediately of this as a physical ailment, but it could have been old age, or grief, or experiences in her past life that broke her spirit and her health.

She is further described as "badly stooped—quite incapable of standing erect." It could also be from what she had to do in order to survive, living as someone's servant or slave that bent her double. Working in fields, cleaning, being a servant or slave would necessitate a bending down position for long periods of time. But Jesus sees her, looking past the others gathered to worship on the Sabbath.

He stops his teaching when he catches sight of her and calls out to her! "Woman, you are free of your infirmity!" He addresses her with the highest mark of respect in the Jewish community. At the sound of his words, everyone in the women's section would have been shocked and startled, wondering if it was she he was addressing so formally and with such admiration. And then we hear that "he laid his hand on her," which means he left the raised platform in the front, went down the middle of the synagogue to touch her at the back of the group, nearly out in the public area. Every woman would have instinctively moved away from him, so that he wouldn't touch them as he passed by.

He laid hands on her. Most people in religious tradition, when asked to lay hands on people, will lay hands on a person's head or their shoulder in prayer of blessing. But she responds immediately to his laying his hand on her, which meant he probably puts his hands under her arms and lifted her up so that she could stand straight for the first time in years.

And she responded and "began thanking God," which meant she probably broke into singing a psalm of deliverance. At that moment Jesus is standing beside her, she prays. Up in the front of the synagogue, the chief priest has tried to get the attention of the people, all of whom are watching the two of them as they worship. The priest is indignant, angry, and chastises everyone but especially Jesus and the woman who stands with him now. Seeking to invalidate Jesus's compassion and tending to her, the priest quotes the law, informing him and the congregation that Jesus broke the law by *working* on the Sabbath.

But Jesus will not allow him to dissuade others from imitating Jesus. Jesus contradicts the chief along with all of those who sit in judgment using strong language: "O you hypocrites! Which of you does not let his ox or his ass out of the stall on the Sabbath to water it? Should not this daughter of Abraham here who has been in the bondage of Satan for eighteen years have been released from her shackles on the Sabbath?" He condemns all of them for not helping her, for treating her shamefully, even treating their animals better than a fellow congregant—animals used for their work and transportation. And then he praises her, as "a daughter of Abraham," which those at the synagogue fail to be, as she is one who professes to obey Abraham and God's covenant.

He describes her condition as bound by Satan. *Bound* here usually means anything hindering a person from living and doing good, anything (or any person) that is an obstacle to being faithful. Yet she has been faithful, even in her suffering and long exclusion from the community and pain.

Jesus in so many words bluntly declares that if we do not free others from their bondage, their suffering and pain, on the other six days of a week, then the best time to do it is the Sabbath, because the Sabbath is the way we free one another, a mark of worshiping our God in whose image we are created.

From the context, we have the sense that Jesus hasn't returned to the front, but continues his preaching standing beside her, in loud protest of the chief priest standing in front and others who add their judgment to the leader's. Then we are also told what, sadly, happens next. "His opponents were covered with confusion; while everyone else rejoiced at the marvels Jesus was accomplishing" (Luke 13:17). The word *confusion* implies anger, being shamed, and strongly convicted. Whenever Jesus does something that sets others free, liberating them and repairing and restoring their lives, we see two different reactions: those opposing his teaching and others who live in recognition and solidarity with his teaching, including those enslaved by sorrow and grief, broken in spirit or living on the edges of society, excluded by others.

Again, in the saying of storytellers everywhere, "The story begins when the teller stops talking." Did Jesus go back in to finish the Sabbath service with everyone else? Did he embrace her and all the others gathering to share in her good news and release? Did he go home with the crowd to celebrate the main meal of the Sabbath in her house and with her friends?

The work, and it is work, of repairing someone's soul begins first seeing, acknowledging, welcoming, and drawing others into a relationship of equals, of community. Words follow: repairing the soul involves proclaiming their goodness, speaking into what their past has been, what they have had to live through, and acknowledging where they are now.

And then the work of repairing the soul continues: we must go out to them, go past others, to where they stand, to touch them and *side* with them as they endeavor to stand up for themselves, believe in themselves, and announce to everyone who they are and how they will live now. Repair of the soul, healing of the soul, involves a continuing relationship, where all involved grow and emerge with new ways of living and relating as God's beloved children, all in the same family.

One of the first and most vital steps in repairing our souls is to tell our stories in a safe place where we are assured there are no interruptions, no questions, no advice, no adding our own bits into their telling: to be listened to with respect, to share our journeys, and to be honored in our sorrows and joys, and to have all understand what we have endured to get to where we stand now.

We can practice how to do this, in telling our own stories and in listening to others' stories, and by practicing listening to our ancestors, our elders, and those who are our mentors, teachers, shamans, chiefs, and those who initiate us and make us leaders in our communities.

Once, after a day of a gathering group where we listened to each other's stories, an elder told the group that to forge our strengths, we must remember that our elders and ancestors gave us more than wounds. They gave us wisdom, insight, and knowledge that we can use now.

We can learn to listen and tell our stories by reading others' tellings, and if we have difficulty speaking in our own voices in the beginning, we can use others' words. And we can also write our stories down, putting our voices, our feelings, fears, experiences, questions, doubts, and emotions on paper, into words. We might write, addressing our own souls and spirits, write to our ancestors or a loved one, write to the Great Spirit, our God who is the Word made flesh. Writing is a prayer that God hears, takes to his heart, drawing us close.

Writing our stories can heal us. As Deena Metzger says, in *Writing for Your Life*: "Stories heal us because we become through them. In the process of writing, of discovering our story, we restore those parts of ourselves that have been scattered, distorted, suppressed, denied, forbidden, and hidden, and we come to understand that stories heal. We are like a broken vessel, and story has the possibility of gathering us up again."

Archbishop (now) Saint Oscar Romero preached to his people telling them, "In the midst of my oppression and captivity, I must never forget that I am the exact imprint of the image of God." Our ancestors and elders constantly remind us of this—of who we are and who we can be.

Along with our ancestors, storytellers, and guardian spirits, we can similarly find wisdom and power to repair our souls in the wisdom of all nature, all of earth, waters, sky, air, and creatures. The world and all that God, the maker and the keeper, has created is laced with energy and spirit. Just being in it heals, repairs, and restores our bodies and souls.

Even seeing photographs of animals, birds, landscapes we have lived in and visited can remind us of restoration, trigger healing, hope, delight that seeps into our memories, thoughts, and actions. Just watching someone, a mother or grandmother, stand or kneel behind a younger relative, holding their hair in their hands, intently braiding and arranging their hair, can stir fixing and repairing something in our hearts. There are moments we see, catch out of the corner of our eyes, that instill respect, and reveal sacredness to us. Everywhere we walk, or stop to look, to really *see*, can make a moment holy. Ojibwe elder Edward Benton-Banai would begin his prayers saying, "Every footstep becomes a prayer."

Chris La Tray, a Metis storyteller, a descendant of the Pembina Band of the Red River of the North, a member of the Little Shell Tribe of Chippewa Indians, writes in his piece "Chasing Spirit," in the December 2022 issue of *Sojourners*, about one of his Sunstack newsletters: "An Irritable Metis." He describes a black and white photograph he has tacked above his computer monitor. It is an image of a small herd of *mashkode-bizhikiwag* buffalo spread out across a grassy plain. It is a rare sight in reality, but the picture brings him peace. How much more is their power, standing and watching as the light changes and they move across the prairie!

In many religious and Indigenous traditions and among ancient peoples, such as those in Ireland, Wales, England, Northern Europe, New Zealand, Australia, and elsewhere, there are wisdom practices related to spirit trees and totem animals or birds who teach us about who we are, our spirits, and how to live with change, growth, sickness, what we carry within us as gifts or weaknesses, and how to be healed and become whole again. There are communal healing rituals but also stories and ways to personally learn from all the other creatures of the universe. Soul Medicine is shared among animals, birds, fish, many creatures, places, and human beings. In many groups there are also naming ceremonies, where we are given *names* other than ones given by family. These names reveal our hidden sparks, our gifts, and spirit. One story related to this comes from Native American storytelling. The story is called Wolf Medicine or Wolf Woman.

It was not so long ago, still told by the older ones. It was when the Blackfoot were moving from their summer to their winter camp. As they were traveling, they were attacked by a band of Crow warriors. Many were killed or wounded. Only a few escaped. One young woman, who was called Sits-By-The-Door was taken captive and kept as a slave.

The captors moved far on their horses, and when they set up winter camp, she was treated harshly, worked hard, insulted, humiliated, sometimes kicked, and shoved to the ground. And she was given rotten food to eat, the discards no one else would eat. She was brought into one of the chief's tents and she slept next to his wife. The wife was good-hearted and kind, and felt pity for her. They didn't know each other's language, but they shared some sign language and would try to speak with each other, and she would bring her bits of food, a piece of clothing, and herbs when she was scratched or feeling sick.

One night the chief's wife whispered to her that they were planning on killing her, but she would help her escape. First, she cut the rawhide strips that bound her hands and feet, rubbing them to get the circulation moving. She had collected a small pouch with food, dried meat, pemmican, herbs, roots to chew on, and a bit of sage. She walked with her, held her for a moment and then stood and watched her run.

Sits-By-The-Door knew she had to keep moving. They would not let her go easily, but rather try to track her. All night she ran, resting for a moment here and there. It was the same the next day. That night as the moon rose and night came, she found a cave, crawled in, and collapsed exhausted. She slept fitfully and ate the last of her gift of food. After three days she knew she had to get up and find food and see where she was and if she could find her home again. She started out, but it was just a few hours into her journey that she realized she was being followed: a wolf was tracking her. She'd stop, lean against a tree, or stand on a rise and watch it following her relentlessly. It was a full-grown wolf, grey with streaks of black. She tried to keep moving during the day and into the night.

But she just couldn't go on. She leaned up against a tree, cried softly and knew the wolf would move on her.

He approached her with care, slowly watching her, stopping to sniff her out. She could smell him, his fur, his breath, his drool. She was terrified. It was a terrible way to die, and she prayed for deliverance. He stood right next to her, sniffing at her clothes and hair. Then to her utter amazement, the wolf lay down beside her, curling up against her, sharing his warmth with her, as though he was guarding her and keeping her safe!

When she awoke, he had slipped away, but he was back soon, before she tried to get up and walk. He was dragging half of a buffalo calf he had killed, putting it at her feet. She struggled up, got firewood and cooked the meat, and they ate it together. This became their new pattern. The wolf would bring back something to cook, or eat, animal or a bird. She collected roots, leaves, sometimes a fish, and they would share their meals. At night the wolf would sleep with her, and during the day they would walk together, the wolf warning her of anything nearby. They were together for several moons, but she finally found her way back to her people's camp. They were surprised that she treated the wolf like a dear friend, but were impressed with her story and how they had cared for one another.

She told her people as they sat around the night fire, with the wolf stretched out beside her: He is strong medicine. He saved my life and helped me learn how to survive and live again, and to find my way home. He is my friend, Medicine Wolf.

The people talked about having a wolf in the camp with them, and the elders told old stories of other animals and birds who had helped some of them, with food, with protection, and plants that could heal disease. They decided the wolf could stay with them and live with Sits-By-The-Door. Strangely, even the dogs quickly learned to live in peace with the wolf. He would go out at times to hunt and bring back what he found that was old, or had died in the wild, and share it with her, as she and others shared their food with the wolf. She lived, alone, for many years, collecting herbs and plants, sharing what she learned on her escape from being a slave and became one of the respected chiefs.

And then she died sleeping next to her wolf friend. He stood outside the village that night and howled long. After that night, he was never seen again.

The story may seem fanciful to some, but there are many accounts of ravens, deer, even seals, porpoises, hawks, all sorts of four-leggeds, ones considered wild, and other creatures befriending humans. These are totem animals that teach us, just by our catching sight of them and watching them as they live.

This is true also of many peoples and trees. It is believed that if you are troubled, trying to discern or decide on something, even just discouraged or lonely, that a tree that grows nearby often within walking distance of you is your spirit tree at that moment. You can recognize it immediately. Then you are to stand by it, study it, listen to it, sit under it, even climb it, look at it from different angles, smell it, even taste the bark and leaves. It will speak and teach you, sharing what you need to know at that moment to return to your life, stronger, more aware, freer, more peaceful, and knowing yourself more intimately. Even sharing your spirit tree with others can help to heal something by its presence and power. It is a rare gift to share your spirit tree, animal, bird, or place with someone else, part of becoming deeper truer friends with another person.

In another healing story, where Jesus gathers the divine sparks, repairing someone's body and soul—we see how the moment of repairing of one's soul also leaves a healing mark or sense on our bodies as well. Often what is directed at the soul comes through, is felt or made visible, in our bodies. This story is found early in Mark's Gospel.

> He returned to the synagogue where there was a man whose hand was shriveled up. They kept an eye

> on Jesus to see whether he would heal him on the Sabbath, hoping to be able to bring an accusation against him. He addressed the man with the shriveled hand: "Stand up here in front!" Then he said to them: "Is it permitted to do a good deed on the Sabbath—or an evil one? To preserve life—or destroy it?" At this they remained silent. He looked around at them with anger, for he was deeply grieved that they had closed their minds against him. Then he said to the man, "Stretch out your hand." The man did so, and his hand was perfectly restored. When the Pharisees went outside they immediately began to plot with the Herodians how they might destroy him. (Mark 3:1–6)

Again, it's Sabbath and Jesus is in the synagogue. This time it looks like there's a setup, where Jesus sees a man with a shriveled hand as some of the Pharisees are trying to trap Jesus so that they can accuse him, and punish him, and thus exclude him from the community. They care nothing for the man. They are using the man to attack Jesus. They "keep an eye on him to see whether he'll heal the man, knowing it's the Sabbath," and knowing Jesus will be breaking that law if he does.

Even in the place of prayer and worship the Pharisees are cold-hearted and plotting. Jesus knows what they're trying to do, but he cares more about the man and his suffering than about what the leaders of the community will do with him.

Jesus tells the man, "Stand up here in front!" That's where Jesus is standing, so he calls him up to stand next to him. But then he turns and confronts the others, questioning them. He posits a fundamental ethical question on behavior and what is good or right and what is evil and wrong. "Is it permitted to do a good deed on the Sabbath" where technically it is breaking the law—or an evil one? In no uncertain terms he says that not to help, that not to care for others on any day of the week, when you do have the capacity to help, is wrong, is evil. He goes on being very specific about the option presented before him and all of them of the choice: "to preserve life—or destroy it?" And they are mute, refusing to respond to him.

This is one of the few times we are told that Jesus looks at anyone with anger, but he does. He's deeply grieved that they have closed their minds against him and that they are so hard-hearted that they care nothing for someone who has suffered long and been excluded from life in so many ways. They are entrenched in their own group and will go to great lengths to keep people subjugated to their judgments and their dictates of how people should live—including Jesus.

But Jesus chooses to stand in solidarity with the man whose hand is shriveled and unresponsive. "Stretch out your hand," Jesus says. And the man obeys, his hand and arm restored. His arm functions again, he can use it now, or can use it with new mobility.

In a sense, Jesus is saying to him: stretch your heart, stretch your soul, stretch your belief in yourself, stretch your belief in me because I will work with you and restore your wholeness, your integrity, and your ability to live. And at the same time, Jesus is saying to those who are trying to trap him, who hold no compassion for the man in need, or anyone else, except themselves, to those retaining their judgments on religious practice and how others are to worship God: to them, also, he is pleading: Stretch your heart, thaw your cold rage, open your mind, melt your animosity, let others' pain touch you, care about others besides yourself, learn compassion. But they do not. In fact, those who oppose the healing of the soul seek out others to band together to ensure they are not cared for or treated with tenderness and respect. They even band together with a group they consider their enemies, the Herodians, to stop Jesus from healing peoples' bodies, minds, and souls.

They will have nothing to do with the fundamental practice of their religion and many others: *tikkun olam*, fixing the world, repairing society, mending relationships, all considered sacred acts, intimately connected to other forms of liturgical worship. They will not gather light or sparks, set others free, liberate people from bondage and what continues to destroy and break down peoples' lives and souls.

The work of *tikkun olam* is work that restores not only one person but ripples out in healing, making our and others' lives whole again. As I once heard the poet Maya Angelou say in a talk, "As soon as healing takes place, go out and heal somebody else." This spiritual practice and work are never really done alone, but rather with others.

And it is part of how we engage, invite, and struggle with others as we repair souls—discovering we too are repaired in the process.

> *The idea of "moving on" from grief implies that mourners experience a loss then leave it behind somewhere. But that's not how it works. How it works is we take our loss by the hand and learn to walk forward with our grief.*
>
> —Alan Wolfelt, *365 Days of Undertanding Your Grief*

INTENTION, REFLECTION, RESPONSE

One of the strongest ways of taking our loss by the hand and moving forward with it is to speak it to others, sharing it.

When we meet the grief of others, we do this, following the pattern that Jesus practices.

First, we look around and see who and what is right here in front of us in pain—often with a pain that has been there for a long period of time, but no one thought to notice, or refused to see.

Then we must cry out, address the person and the situation as Jesus does, with respect, personal connection, and an announcement of hope, akin to Jesus's words "Woman, you are freed from your infirmity!"

Next, we must move toward the people and the place where they stand, go out to them, and stand alongside them in solidarity. We must do this, even if it means going through others, as we decide with whom we will stand.

Finally, we touch them, lift them up, support them, remain near them as they find their voice and begin their first steps into the way forward.

Who have you been vaguely aware is suffering but you ignored them, or refused to become involved with them, carelessly allowing them to struggle to continue on their own, and in doing so, added to their suffering by your disdain for them?

Whenever someone or a group is struggling to heal and to repair their souls, there are inevitably those who ignore them, those who become obstacles to their healing, those who through fear or selfishness stand in their way, lacking compassion or worse, distrust and disdain. To those, Jesus responds in both anger and sadness. In anger he is impelled to speak the truth, to confront those who do evil in their reactions to others, or who refuse to help others when they can. In Judaism it is considered a sin to refuse to give aid and comfort or help someone in need when you are aware of their situation. Part of sharing in others' pain is defending them against others who are callous or unresponsive. We must learn to stand with those in need, understanding that this may demand our standing against, in opposition to, others who are not helping those in pain.

Connected to this, in dealing with sustained trauma and violence across generations, is the issue of taking responsibility for the consequences of the behavior and actions of our ancestors. Just as we must rely on those who have gone before us in faith to learn how to live as those who believe in God among us, we must also take responsibility for those living before who destroyed God's image in others. As their descendants, we must do justice and seek to undo the harm that they did, that we, in turn, had a share in.

The prophet Nehemiah lived in the period known as the Restoration, when he with others sought to rebuild the walls of Jerusalem and introduced administrative reforms to enable the community to begin to live again.

Nehemiah begins his chronicle speaking about the "remnant of Jews preserved after their captivity." They were "survivors, living under great distress and under reproach." The city itself was in ruins, and Nehemiah, like Jesus the prophet, "began to weep and continued mourning for several days; I fasted and prayed before the God of heaven." His prayer in Nehemiah 1:5–11 speaks of confessing the sins of the Israelites, the people who have been faithless, committing sins against God by breaking the commandments during their history, in their past. The people are described as "grievously offending God," but Nehemiah reminds them that God will bring them back together to their dwelling place. He is clear in testifying "that both my forefathers' house and I have sinned" (Nehemiah 1:5).

He prays for strength to rebuild the city walls, do the hard work of reopening the gates, and repair the sectors of the city in need of rebuilding. He includes a list of all the specific places that need work. And he rails against those who refuse to do the work and who ridicule those seeking to enact the restorations (Nehemiah 3:33–38).

In spite of those in opposition to Nehemiah and others, they "worked with a will." The entire book deals pragmatically and practically with the obstacles others put before them in an attempt to stop their repairing and rebuilding their places in the world. And, as with all prophets, Nehemiah sees his voicing anger has people turning against him. But he stays with the people, encouraging them, as he joins them in the daily work of restoration.

Consider, what groups in our own lives do we need to remember—from both our present realities and inherited histories? And what actions do we need to take together to repair the harm done that continues to affect people today—among the historical harms, we see Native Americans, First Nations, Asian, Black, and brown communities, immigrant populations and minority groups calling for repair?

This work of repairing our souls can begin—and can take quantum leaps—as we return to or start a new work in any of the arts: it may be writing, music, dancing, playing an instrument, drumming, drawing, painting, photography, beading, weaving, quilting, making pottery, sewing clothing. We can go to the earth for repair, making gardens of herbs for medicine, flowers for joy, and food for cooking and feeding others, eaten together with others. Any of these activities when done with others heals, restores, repairs, and re-creates us in beauty, wholeness, and grace.

When I traveled, often in Central and South America, staying with families who shared their food, beds, and hospitality with me, I was often met by the children as I went to bed at night. They would assemble around where I would be sleeping and sometimes, they would sing to me, or we would say our night prayers together. And many times, I would be given a small gift to place beside what served as my pillow. I would be given a tiny box, painted with bright colors, red, green, and yellow mostly, with a lid. The box was opened and tiny simply exquisite dolls were taken out and lined up. Little men, women, children, animals, and things I was unsure what they were!

These were carefully put before me. I was told they were *worry dolls*. I was to take each one, tell it a trouble or worry, and put it back into the box. There were always at least five or six and sometimes eight or more. When they were all safely back in the box, one of the children would put the top back on and declare, "OK, now you can go to sleep. They'll take care of all your troubles for the night."

The box then would go under a pillow or blanket, and after hugs all around, I'd be set for the night. The tiny box of handmade dolls, the ritual, and the children all served to heal a troubled spirit and restore peace so that all of us could rest and sleep better that night. They gave me memories I have never forgotten. In the words often attributed to Robert Louis Stevenson, "Like a bird singing in the rain, let grateful memories survive in time of sorrow."

10

Tikkun Olam: Repairing Relationships

No medicine is more valuable, none more efficacious, none better suited to the cure of all our temporal ills than a friend to whom we may turn for consolation in times of trouble and with whom we may share our happiness in times of joy.

—Aelred of Rievaulx

In the center of the Universe dwells the Great Spirit—that center is really everywhere. It is within each one of us.

—Black Elk

Tikkun olam is a reality that operates and is practiced on a number of levels, personally and individually, with another person, in small intentional groups, and in groups that radiate into all areas of our lives: religiously, economically, racially, nationally, tribally, and across all boundaries of the human family.

Tikkun olam seeks to gather souls and bring them together more closely, even intimately. It is a restorative practice that undoes the harm that we have done, and the harm we have experienced from others, re-creating newness and possibilities of life with others held in grace, in harmony, and in peace. That's when, as theologian Walter Brueggemann said, "Newness happens in the world when long-silenced people get their voice enough to sing dangerous alternatives." This is one of the many ways we repair each other's worlds.

Repairing relationships takes a lifetime. But to seriously work at such restoration and repair brings beauty, peace, delight, freedom, and wholeness to all parties. There is an amazing story from the traditions of Asia that reveals this restoration process to us and shows us how it moves us into new areas of experience and knowledge. It's a story that shows us that our attitude toward others and what we seek in relationships of healing always bring forth beauty.

Once upon a time a workman in a palace was collecting his tools. Tired and worn from his long day's labor, he turned and accidentally hit a priceless vase that fell from the table and shattered into pieces. He was terrified. The emperor was enraged. The poor man barely escaped with his life. The emperor decided to offer a magnificent reward to anyone who could put the vase back together in such a way that it was not immediately noticeable that it had been destroyed.

The pieces were carefully collected in a box. And the word went forth that anyone skilled in making or repairing pots would be rewarded if they could *fix* and repair the vase. A long line of people presented themselves, and they tried, they really tried, but no one could effectively repair the vase. First there were all the pieces: it was like trying to put a jigsaw puzzle together. They even had people try to draw it from memory so they knew what it looked like before. Other vases that were of the same era were brought forward for comparison. Even the one that was its matching pair was presented. Now they knew what it could look like repaired. But no one was skilled enough to do it.

The emperor grew angry and the word went forth that anyone else who tried to repair the vase and failed would be executed. That quickly stopped the parade of would-be fixers. There was, in the kingdom, an old monk who dwelled in a cave in the mountains on the edge of the city. Word came to him and to everyone's surprise (and his disciples' dismay) he came to the city and the palace of the emperor, asking to see the pieces so that he could repair the vase. But he insisted on taking the pieces back with him to where he lived and working on it away from the palace. His request was granted, and he and his apprentice took the pieces and returned home.

Off the monk went into his cave, into a back area alone. His apprentice would visit him, sit and talk with him, pray with him, take walks with him, share his meals, and sleep nearby. The weeks went on, and the monk kept at his work on the pieces of the vase.

Finally, he asked his disciple to look at his work and see what he thought. Was it good enough to return to the palace? Could the cracks and pieces missing, or chipped be noticed? Would people want to examine it carefully to see if it really was *that* broken vase? His apprentice didn't know what to say: it was, in a word, lovely. Beautiful. Exquisite. Flawless.

So, off they went on their journey back to the city, to present the vase to the emperor. He was delighted! It was gorgeous. It looked just like the original. He couldn't tell the difference. He examined it closely for faded colors where there would have been a merging of the broken shards and couldn't find any. And so, the monk was graciously rewarded and they returned home, leaving the vase behind in its old place, now in a niche where it could be admired by anyone passing by.

The monk went back to his old routine and so did his apprentice and the other disciples, and eventually they once again concentrated on their daily tasks. But one day, the apprentice was cleaning up the old monks' quarters and he found a pile of broken pieces. Then he found another cache in a corner under some stones! There were many fragments! He ran to the monk, bringing some of them with him, screaming at him: "Look at all these broken pieces! You never used them when you reassembled the vase! How could you do that? How come you have all these old broken bits?" He, and others who heard the commotion were excited, angry, feeling betrayed, cheated, dismayed by how he did it, and in awe of the finished repaired vase.

The monk quieted them all down and said simply, "If you do this kind of work—repair what is shattered and broken—if you do this work with love, with attentiveness, with respect and patience—it will always become something of grace and beauty. Your soul will guide you to the other's soul, even just in their pieces, and it will remember its wholeness and come back together again."

We may think this story is an impossibility, like a Zen parable that teaches by undoing what we usually think and feel, throwing us into the unknown, into mystery. But there are stories in the gospel of relationships people have with Jesus that show this repair in equally amazing ways. Take this version of a story that appears halfway through Matthew's Gospel, in chapter 15. It takes place after the Pharisees and scribes question Jesus as to why "he acts contrary to the tradition of our ancestors." He tries to teach the disciple and the other people nearby what the difference is between what areas of life need to be changed and those that remain whole and helpful in life and practice. But he is not received well, and so we read, "Then Jesus left that place and withdrew to the district of Tyre and Sidon." Jesus leaves Israel and enters foreign territory. The word used to describe his departure and where he goes is withdraw. It is a word used in military actions to convey needing to back up, retreat, and reconnoiter before continuing a course of action. Here is the story.

> It happened that a Canaanite woman living in that locality presented herself, crying out to him, "Lord,

> Son of David, have pity on me! My daughter is terribly troubled by a demon." He gave her no word in response. His disciples came up and began to entreat him: "Get rid of her. She keeps shouting after us!" "My mission is only to the lost sheep of the house of Israel," Jesus replied [to them]. She came forward then and did him homage with the plea: "Help me, Lord!" But he answered, "It is not right to take the food of the sons and daughters and throw it to the dogs." "Please, Lord," she insisted, "even the dogs eat the leavings that fall from their masters' tables." Jesus then said in reply, "Woman, you have great faith! Your wish will come to pass." That very moment her daughter got better. Jesus left that place and passed along the Sea of Galilee. (Matthew 15:1–4ff. and 21–29)

Many people find this story disconcerting and try to interpret it so that Jesus doesn't come off looking rude, insensitive—even racist—and interpret his response as his way of relating to her spiritually, by testing her faith before he gives her what she desperately needs, forcing her to beg him for her daughter's life. We think, *this is a human being, Jesus.* Yet, Jesus, a Jew, is acting as other Jews of his time, place, and background. He has left Israel and is in the territory of Gentiles, unbelievers, and still she approaches him and calls him "Lord, Son of David," a specifically Jewish title.

He has left his home country in part because his own

people refuse to listen to him, rejecting his words and criticizing his behavior. This Canaanite woman, however, in her desperateness will take help from anyone, including someone considered an enemy, a gentile in a territory the Israelites conquered, taking a land they considered the *promised land* away by occupation.

She trails along behind him and his disciples, crying out, making a scene, focusing the attention of bystanders on Jesus, and begging him for help. She's direct and to the point in her need. She calls him Lord, Son of David—something even his own people are reluctant to do—and she asks for his *pity* on behalf of her daughter who is suffering. The child is "terribly troubled by a demon," she says. This troubling can suggest any number of ailments and diseases that attack one's nervous system, causing fits, convulsions, passing out, fainting. But these issues might also be symptomatic of young children suffering from slow persistent starvation, a frequent cause of death for many newborns and young children across the Middle East at the time of Jesus. Whatever the exact issue, the child's growth and her ability to just survive were threatened.

We don't expect Jesus's response. First, we're surprised that he says nothing, does not respond to her, and ignores her. We often miss the background sounds, that in fact the disciples are quick to respond and loud in their efforts to be rid of her. In their eyes she does not deserve to even be acknowledged by Jesus. She's not one of them.

They ask Jesus to shut her up, make her go away. They are in a foreign country, uncomfortable themselves, and they likely don't want anyone making them publicly known. But she will not let up, and she is persistent, loud, and demanding.

Jesus speaks to his disciples, telling them who he is and what he's been trying to do in his own country, as she overhears his remark. "My mission is only to the lost sheep of the house of Israel." This has been his work since he began his preaching in his home town—and he has been consistently not believed, and often outright rejected and contradicted by those nearest to him.

She doesn't accept his *teaching*, continues her cries and *does him homage*, upping the ante. This means that she got down on her hands and knees, crawled up to him, most likely wrapping her arms around his legs, begging for his attention and response.

This time Jesus responds. And we find his words off-putting, insensitive—not like our often milk-toast image of Jesus. He uses contemporary language of the Jewish people to describe gentiles as *unclean, outsiders, pagans.* "It is not right to take the food of sons and daughters and throw it to the dogs," Jesus says. This is exactly what the disciples were thinking. Jesus voices their feelings about her and the people of the land he is now visiting.

But she's quick, desperate, and knows Jesus is Jewish, but she also knows he cares about others: the poor, diseased, lame, blind, even lepers of his own people, and he helps them because he is compassionate—putting into practice what he preaches. So, she comes back at him: "Please, Lord," still respectfully insisting, "even the dogs eat the leavings that fall from their masters' tables." If she must act like a dog with a master, she will. If Jesus is a master in his own household, among his own people, she'll get herself connected to him, anyway she can. She hopes he will respond. She shocks him as surely as Jesus's words shock us.

And she got to him. Jesus is taken aback, stunned by her daring approach to him, when she professes who he is: Lord, Son of David, master, as she brings to him the great love she has for her child that she likens to his own love for the least of God's beloved children. "Woman" he responds, using the highest form of respect in his community, "you have great faith!" In a sense he is saying, respected woman, you're just like me in your love of others in need. "Your wish will come to pass." Or as other translations say, "It will be done unto you according to your word."

What happened next? Did Jesus bend down to her and lift her up as he sent her on her way back to her child? He simply tells her to go home. And the scene is given a postscript to the story: we are told the child gets better. How? Does the healing and repairing of the child's body and soul start in that moment and then continue as she heals and grows stronger and healthier? And what does she do? Or how do the others respond to this scene? We do not hear from her again, but the story is told—the readers are given the story's healing events. In the scriptures, that return to the fulfillment of her story and her "wish" suggests she and her family have now become followers of Jesus, part of his community, even disciples.

What is the reaction or response of the disciples? He has broken major laws now, moving outside all the traditions and teachings of the Jewish people, the law, and the covenant. He's gone way beyond his earlier argument around the Sabbath traditions, traditions around washing of hands, what is pure and impure, allowed or condemned, including interaction with someone who isn't Jewish.

In that moment Jesus changes, radically alters who he believes himself to be, what his mission and work is, and what his future will be. He belongs to the world now. One woman—seen as an enemy of his own people, an outsider, stranger, gentile, unclean person—taught him and revealed to him who he is and why he is in the world. He heals and sets in motion her child's restoration and future, and he shifts his own understanding of himself and why he is God's beloved child.

The Incarnation has been extended to God becoming flesh—all flesh, not just one nation or one group of people. He has learned from her . . . how to be Jesus!

From there the Gospel of Matthew continues, reinforcing this moment of insight, conversion, and becoming. Jesus now goes to a mountain outside Israel, and when large crowds come to him, he begins to heal and restore them *all*—those who are crippled, blind, and lame; those who have deformations, those who are mute—and many others besides. Those who witness the change on the mountain respond, "They glorified the God of Israel." Jesus now belongs, and his mission expands to the world.

This story introduces us to a moment Jesus is transformed and changed *as much as* those he encounters and heals—much in the same way we might interact with others who have long known trauma, violence, and suffering that impacts their very survival. And ultimately, we are changed. Yes, we, like the disciples and Jesus, may be slow or reluctant to meet, to connect with those we know are so different from us, so broken in our eyes. Maybe differences may not be immediately noticeable, and we may not be aware of their situations, but we may discover we are very conscious of their differences and what they are struggling with, too. Antoine de Saint-Exupéry said, "He who is different from me does not impoverish me—he enriches me." This is our starting point when we decide to relate to others living with the effects and consequences of violence, trauma, and the dislocation of their bodies and souls.

We can begin to interact and relate to others with grace and healing, to repair others' lives as individuals, but it is much easier, and more common to participate in repair in community. As the song sings, "I get by with a little help from my friends." Being a friend with others is the usual way we participate in the marvelous work of repairing relationships with others who are in need, who are traumatized, broken, afraid, paralyzed, depressed and living in misery—whether or not they hide it well.

PTSD (post-traumatic stress disorder), as it's called in counseling and in the psychology community, is the sometimes hidden but ongoing trauma that is retriggered for so many, even long after the original events. But there also is what may follow when we try to live with grace and wholeness once again: dubbed PTG, or post-traumatic growth. This growth is a change in radically positive ways. PTSD afflicts the survivors of war, violence, and personal and social trauma related to racism, sexism, and religious hatred. It is part of the makeup of those presently struggling with these issues, but it is also found in the children and grandchildren, generations that bear the burdens and memories of their parents' and ancestors' experiences of violence. It is seeded in their histories, memories, character traits, even in their genes.

And PTG is about finding, creating, and trying out old and new actions, patterns, and experiences connected and born out of knowledge, counsel, religious beliefs, and understandings that engage healing and growth. That healing is spreading to other cultures, religious groups and those who have been in the military, racial groups, as slaves, minorities who were excluded, persecuted, and affected by political, economic, and religious trauma and violent experiences individually and in groups. In life-affirming, life-giving, imaginative, creative, positive ways, PTG is the result of tending to old wounds, and starting healthy, restorative patterns of behavior, thought, and interactions with others.

One time, after being with a group of children between six and nine years old, where we were reading Dr. Seuss, one of them said, "I know what we're talking about! It's Dr. Seuss, in my book *The Lorax*, he says: 'It's not about what is, it's about what it can become.' " Exactly.

A story that reminds us of this becoming is found in both Mark's and Matthew's Gospels. The text below appears very early in Mark's Gospel (2:1–12), right after Jesus begins his mission and ministry, in response to his baptism, in the power of the Spirit.

> He came back to Capernaum after a lapse of several days and word got around that he was at home. At that they began to gather in great numbers. There was no longer any room for them, even around the door. While he was delivering God's Word to them, some people arrived bringing a paralyzed man to him. The four who carried him were unable to bring him to Jesus because of the crowd, so they began to open up the roof over the spot where Jesus was. When they had made a hole, they let down the mat on which the paralytic was lying. When Jesus saw their faith, he said to the paralyzed man, "My son, your sins are forgiven!" (Mark 2:1–5)

We can see the setup and the lengths this paralyzed man's friends were willing to go to get to Jesus and get their friend close enough to him so that they could interact. Jesus returns to Capernaum, a town on the seacoast where all kinds of people would be passing through in their daily lives. This is where Jesus makes his home-away-from-home when he is no longer welcome in Nazareth. And he's surrounded by the crowds.

But this man's friends are ingenious. They check the

house out, go around the back, away from the crowds in front (usually one side was open to the street). And they climb up on the roof. It's a good size, well-constructed house, with a tiled roof. They remove a section of tiles, open a space, and the four of them get the man on his mat up on the roof and maneuver him over the opening.

Then the four of them lower him on the mat so that he lands on the ground in front of Jesus. We can imagine Jesus beginning to notice what they are doing (along with others inside and the owners of the house!). They look up, watching and probably enjoying every moment, delighted with the depth of love shown by the friends of the man they are hoping Jesus will see and touch. We are told that Jesus does look up at the man's friends and sees "their faith"—their love, and how much they are willing to share their friend with him, in spite of his affliction and inability to get to Jesus. The story continues.

> When he saw their faith, he said to the paralyzed man: "My son, your sins are forgiven." Now some of the scribes were sitting there asking themselves: "Why does this man talk in that way? He commits blasphemy! Who can forgive sins except God alone?" Jesus was immediately aware of their reasoning, though they kept it to themselves, and he said to them: "Why do you harbor these thoughts? Which is easier, to say to the paralytic, 'Your sins are forgiven,' or to say 'Stand up, pick up your mat, and walk again'? That you may know that the Son of Man

> has authority on earth to forgive sins [turning to the paralytic], "I command you: Stand up! Pick up your mat and go home." The man stood and picked up his mat and went outside in the sight of everyone. They were awestruck; all gave praise to God, saying: "We have never seen anything like this!" (Mark 3:6–12)

Amazing! First Jesus forgives his sins. Recall the word *sin* means *to miss the mark*. It connotes loss, missing something essential, revealing something that needs to be made whole again. In English the word *forgive* comes from the old English, meaning to give, grant, or bestow. It is closely connected to the Hebrew word for gift—something given freely, an offering.

God forgiving our sins in Jesus is his offering to us—the gift of wholeness, of holiness, of healing, and release from our *dis-ease*, from something we lack now being filled, an ability restored. This is what we mean when we acknowledge that at our root, we are all flawed, we are all sinners, in need of forgiveness and restoration to fullness of life.

That's where Jesus begins, calling him son, child, and restoring his relationship with God—and assuring him he is made in God's image, holy and sacred in his sight. You're forgiven. You're in relationship with God, with others; and you, yourself, are created to be whole, to be human.

And as Jesus speaks the words of wholeness and forgiveness, immediately some scribes in the house, seated on the floor, up against the wall, probably across from

Jesus, react. Their minds and hearts immediately accuse Jesus of blasphemy—he can't forgive, only God can. They think nothing of the man, only of rites, of laws and forms that must be obeyed, and even who can forgive sins. Jesus knows them well and verbalizes their antagonism. "Why do you harbor these thoughts?" And he puts the two options before them clearly, making them choose.

Is it easier to say the words and give the gift of forgiveness to another human being? Or is it easier to tell someone to stand up, walk, and go back into your life and live in freedom and hope?

We don't have the response of the Pharisees—it stays in their minds and hearts—but we have the sense that they do not for a moment think that Jesus can do either: forgive sins or to set the man free, giving him the ability to walk again.

Once when I was preaching on this story, I asked those gathered which of the two is easier to do? A young boy, maybe ten, piped up loudly: "I know! I know!! It's harder to forgive. I know because I have to do it with my sister all the time!" There was an outburst of laugher from the congregation, but what he said gets to the heart of what is true.

The man walks again, literally, physically, but he also *stands up*. This word is a theological one, always used to speak of resurrection, of living together in the freedom of the children of God. So, he stands and walks now in the way of Jesus, the way of holiness, in communication and communion with God and with others.

This is the work and continuing experience of healing

and PTG–growth after violence and trauma–that has moments of forgiveness, reminders of who each person is, and the power and spirit/soul lying dormant or buried inside them. And what is dormant or harmed within is now called forth. Those seeking repair are told again who they really are and what they can become again, and they are made anew.

The compassion of the four friends accompany him in meeting Jesus or someone who can tell them what they need to hear, help them see and accept who they are along with what has happened to them and that they do not have to be consumed or paralyzed by their past and what has happened to them or what they have done in order to survive. We are to be such good friends as the four who worked so hard to get him to the person, the help he needed, and we are to be like Jesus, forgiving, encouraging, challenging and urging them forward so that they can walk again, live again with dignity, in freedom and connection with others that is healthy, with integrity and equality.

A note on curing versus healing might be helpful in looking at what we mean when we are talking about PTG–growth and healing from the many effects of violence and trauma that we carry within our bodies and souls, with others mostly unaware of our *dis*-ease, suffering and pain. We'll begin with the word *religion*, which means to bind together, hold together, all of life: body, mind, soul, relations, decisions, etc. It is related to the word used in biology and medical terms to describe sinews, muscles, and veins held together around knees, elbows, the spine, etc. When they are all together, they constitute a wholeness, all of a piece, something that is holy. And they allow the body, soul, and heart freedom of movement.

The word *cure* means to restore to health: to get rid of (a disease or troublesome condition); to preserve (meat, fruit, tobacco, skins); the substance or treatment that cures a disease, a remedy. Originally it meant *looking after* with care, concern, and responsibility (in particular, spiritual care; though it developed into the notion of successful medical care). Now, it often means remission. Someone once said, "We are not cured of living or dying."

The word *heal* (of sore or wounded parts), means to form healthy flesh again, to unite after being cut or broken; to cause to do this . . . the old use was *to heal the sick*. Originally it meant *to make whole* or to restore to sound health. Healing is now seen as an ongoing process, as in actions and decisions taken before, during, and beyond what will be, as opposed to a cure. Healing means to soothe, ease, facilitate, give meaning to, enhance life (body/soul/mind/spirit) in the midst of suffering, pain, *dis*-ease, and illness. It involves the spectrum of living with loss and lack while transforming one's life and situation as well as living with grace and wholeness. Faith can either enhance and be a positive factor in healing practice or be negative, debilitating, and disabling factors in healing.

It is helpful to include a look at the word and meaning of *health*. Health is a state of being well and free from illness; the condition of the body, healthy—beneficial, functioning well—and it is closely related to religion. The practice of integrative medicine today seeks to offer the promise of living a good life, though it may not aways be easy or even long. It is one thing to cure the body; it is another to work at restoring the concept of healing to the heart of health care, recognizing the potential for wholeness in everyone in all situations and stages of living and dying. Integrative medicine is seen as important for the health care professionals as well as those they treat and serve, with others–a mutual strengthening. Rachel Naomi Remen is a doctor, healer, and teacher who writes about this concept for both doctors and the people they interact with in the healing process. In her March 2012 piece "The Recovery of the Sacred" for Context Institute, she wrote this short assessment as a poem.

O body! For 35 years
And 1,573 experts with
14,372 combined years of training
Have failed to cure your wounds.
Deep inside
I
Am whole.

A visible image of this kind of healing in integrative medicine and PTG is the ritual of making and using a Navajo sand painting, which creates a world, putting the *dis*-eased or sick person in that world, sitting on the ground within the painting, with the community around them and interacting with everyone. Then the person gets up and walks back into their world, and the sand painting is destroyed. This is also akin to paintings created in Tibetan rituals.

The process of healing, especially after the experience of violence and trauma is communal. The need for others, and the amount of energy and work that goes into just getting things in position so that something can happen, and the integral nature of healing body/soul/mind and spirit together, as well as the effect it has on those who seek to help heal the person and the larger community, too, is all engaging. It is hard work, and it is not always what we would deem *successful*. We need to look at healing in its larger context: we will all die, but hopefully we will die as we have lived–wholistically, holy, still connected vibrantly to the community, our family and friends, and with God.

INTENTION, REFLECTION, RESPONSE

> *Cows run away from the storm while the buffalo charges toward it and gets through it quicker. Whenever I'm confronted with a tough challenge, I do not prolong the torment. I become the buffalo.*
>
> —Wilma Mankiller, first woman chief of the Cherokee nation

This aptly describes both the people who suffer from PTSD and who are on the journey of healing (PTG) as well as all those involved in interacting with them in healing relationships. For you, what does it mean to "become the buffalo"?

> *God whispers in our pleasure; He talks in our conscience; He shouts in our pain.*
>
> —C. S. Lewis

This is an experience that we know both individually and collectively. Finding someone to share and be respectful of our pain is essential. Do you have someone, or a few trusted souls in your life, to speak of your pain with? Sometimes it may be a counselor, an elder, a priest or shaman, a psychologist, teacher, or a close friend. It can even, on occasion be a stranger that we find ourselves with over a short period of time. In all situations it is a place and time of shared blessings and grace, with God as a witness who listens with us.

There is a marvelous simple story in a 1997 Buena Vista Ink article "The Mirrors of Community" by Anita Kennedy recording an event that happened in Sierra Leone. Anita Kennedy, a Maryknoll missionary, was returning back to her home village, with her red backpack. She was met at the edge of the village by a gaggle of children yelling at her (some of them up in the trees). "Sister, sister, come and snap we!" They knew she carried her camera with her everywhere. She took a picture of all of them up in the tree. She sent the film back to her brother who developed the film and mailed it back to her with a copy of the photo for each child. They gathered around, each with their copy of the photo and immediately began identifying each other. One of them, Mohammed, got every one of them correct. But he didn't find himself! His mother gently pointed out one of the young children, and said, "Mohammed, this now you." He did not recognize himself. There were no mirrors in the village. He was known by his mother, family, friends, and others in the village, but he did not know himself. The people were their human mirrors.

This is what we are for others! Human mirrors. We have the honor, the responsibility, and the possibility of revealing someone to themselves. Who are the persons who do this for you already? Are you looking for someone or others who can reveal you to yourself, and open up possibilities for growth, healing, and new ways of living? Are you this mirror for others? What can you do to be this for others?

> *One of the most vital ways we sustain ourselves is by building communities of resistance, places where we know we are not alone.*
>
> —bell hooks

Do you belong to a community that sustains you? Our church has always been sustained and built on small communities (called Base Christian Communities, BCCs). They are small groups of believers who study the scriptures for conversion, encouraging one another, using the Sunday readings (especially the gospels and prophets) weekly to examine their own lives and together be converted to the gospel and put into practice what they discover in their sharing of understanding the scriptures. You only need about five people to have your sustaining, healing, encouraging group of "the friends of God" to help you grow in faith and become followers of Jesus more deeply.

There is a short vignette from the Jewish tradition recorded by Martin Buber in his *Tales of the Hasidim*. "News was brought to Rabbi Moshe Leib that his friend the rabbi of Berditchev had fallen ill. On the Sabbath, he said his name over and over and prayed for his recovery. Then he put on new shoes made of Moroccan leather, laced them up tight and danced! A zaddik (teacher) who was present said, "Power flowed forth from his dancing. Every step was a power mystery. An unfamiliar light suffused the house, and everyone watching saw the heavenly hosts join the dance!"

This tradition of dancing as prayer, both solo and with others, is shared by First Nations and many Indigenous communities. It is a form of strong prayer for those dancing and for others they draw into their minds and hearts, using their bodies to pray for, as they dance. The drummers dance by providing the music, the beats that set the pace and provide spirit and energy to hold the dancers together. Even those who silently watch, engage, and pray along with the dancers. The sound of the drum is the heartbeat of the earth, of the universe, and all who are present. DANCE! Make music, attend to those who are present, hearing the sounds of healing, comfort, and encouragement. DANCE!

It is important for us to stay in touch with the suffering of the world . . . in order to keep compassion alive in us. . . . And when our hearts awaken, even small gestures can have an immense effect. . . . One word

> *can give comfort and confidence, destroy doubt, help someone avoid a mistake, reconcile a conflict or open the door to liberation. One action can save a person's life or help him take advantage of a rare opportunity. One thought can do the same, because thoughts always lead to words and actions. With compassion in our heart, every thought, word and deed can bring about a miracle.*
>
> —Thich Nhat Hanh

Try a resolution of one single act, gesture, or word of compassion to share with someone every day. And beside doing this with someone you know, be sure you choose someone you do not really know as well each day. Then resolve to do this each time you are in a conversation or discussion with others. Compassion comes from two words: *Com*, meaning with, and *passion* meaning deep feeling (gut feeling) shared with another. The feeling always provokes action. If someone would ask you if you are a compassionate person—how would you respond to them? How could you be specific in relating how and to whom? Who, in your life has treated you with compassion?

11

Tikkun Olam: Healing Structures and Institutions

I will not tire of declaring what we really want is an effective end to violence; we must remove the violence that lies at the root of all violence: structural violence, social injustice, exclusion of citizens from the management of the country, repression. All of this is what constitutes the present cause, from which all the rest flows naturally.

—Oscar Romero

It took me a long time to understand how systems inflict pain and hardship in people's lives and learn that being kind in an unjust system is not enough.

—Helen Prejean

The concept of *tikkun olam* has many layers and intersects with different understandings (theological, philosophical, mystical as well as informing living faith, communities, and the way we practice justice and restoration). In the mystical traditions of Judaism, it figures into the account of creation, where we can see its implications. God contracted himself to make room for creation. The first humans were created to restore the divine sparks scattered when the vessels that tried to contain them shattered and broke. Now the universe is filled with broken sparks of divine light that need to be uncovered, gathered, and restored to the vessel—the way the world was meant to be before it was shattered. This is one layer of what it means to "repair the world."

Another way to understand what *tikkun olam* means is to understand it as actions taken in the social sphere by humans, individuals, and communities in programs that work through changing social issues. These are a gathering of the sparks. This kind of repair re-creates the world and creates history that undoes the harm that affects all aspects of the life of individuals, groups, and nations.

Tikkun olam is reflected in those actions through which society is improved: public policies, laws, institutions, structures, organizations, international bodies, peacemaking, change, restitution, atonement, and creating possibilities that restore the sacred initial wholeness of the world and the way it was meant to function. This includes addressing problems of society such as immigration, slavery, racism, nationalism, violence, sexism, and other isms that harm others. It also includes addressing such issues as food insecurity, inadequate health care, housing deficits, unequal educational opportunities, poverty and economic issues, work production, and problems connected to the earth, air, fire/energy, water, and our natural resources.

Tikkun olam is a way of understanding that deep ruptures and destructive forces have evolved in the universe, and they, along with their consequences, must be undone, repaired, and restored to positive growth and power. As Rabbi Lynn Gottlieb once said in a talk referencing the *Tisha B'av* (Moral Torah) about dealing with violence and our place in the world: "It is not enough to mourn; mourning must be accompanied by actions that end the harm being done."

In Christian theological terms, *tikkun olam* is the bringing about of the Good News to the Poor. It is the building, uncovering, and sustaining the kin-dom of God. It is creating the world of the Beatitudes that Jesus—the Word of God made flesh—preached, bringing into the world by his presence, the healing mystery of the Incarnation. *Tikkun olam* is about creating the Community of Beloved Disciples, so that everyone understands they are Friends of God.

This repairing of society can and must be practiced on an individual level and in communities as well as in the larger society.

For substantial changes to happen in society, it requires understanding how the decisions we make now have long-range consequences, and that change entails our commitments to reformation, life-repairing habits, decisions, and relationships.

These life-restoring habits become lifelong ways of acting and living, and they affect us and our communities. That requires that the initial decisions that ripple through society be based on doing justice, restoring life, and undoing harm that has been done to others.

There is an amazing and terrible story Gandhi told someone who came to him trying to decide how to live with the harmful effects of something he had done—though he was one of many in a group who had brought about harm. I first saw the story in the movie *Gandhi*, and later read an account of it, and I retell it here in my own words.

India had just gained its independence from Britain in 1947. But there were great divisions and strife among groups of Muslims, Hindus, and the British. Killings among factions continued in many areas across India. Gandhi began a fast to try to convince all sides to stop the violence, the brutal outbreaks of rage, and attacks on one another, and begin to come together. For weeks Gandhi continued the fast, becoming noticeably weak from hunger, as he showed signs of dying from starvation.

It was at that time he was visited by a Hindu man who begged him to stop, screaming at Gandhi that he must eat and live. He screamed at him: "I am going to hell—but not with your death on my soul."

Then Gandhi answered: "Only God decides who goes

to hell." Then the man responded with a confession, in front of all the onlookers: "I killed a child!"

"Why?" Gandhi asks.

The man's voice cracked in grief and rage, telling him, "Because they killed my son! The Muslims killed my son!"

Gandhi listened to the man's grief and agony and sensed how hard it was for the man to live with what he has done. But how does anyone undo that kind of harm, or atone for killing?

Gently he told the man, "There is a way out of hell. Find a child, an orphan, someone whose family has been killed—if possible a boy child around the same age as your son—and take him in and raise him as your own son. The only thing I ask is that you find a child who is Muslim." The man listened, almost collapsing in relief. Yes, he could do this and make restitution, raising a child to replace not only his own son but the one he took by killing.

He started to nod in assent, but Gandhi added one more sentence, telling the man, "Remember, though, you must raise him as a Muslim!" Now the man was shocked and fell to his knees. No, not this! This was too much to ask.

Yet, this direction was one of true restoration, of doing justice and repairing what has been so violently destroyed. Not only is the man told to give life in return for the one taken, but to make it a life that closely resembles the life of the child he killed.

The Hindu man must replace the human being who

was a Muslim whose life he shattered with one who grows up with Muslim traditions and bound closely to other Muslims. He himself can remain Hindu, but he must restore the tear in the Muslim community.

We are not told if the Hindu man who confessed to Gandhi and heard his counsel, followed through and obeyed. But he knew the wisdom of acting for restoration at the level of community and in communion with those he harmed so grievously.

We also know the extent and depth of what is entailed in restoring the harm and undoing the violence we have been part of. We have some sense of the radical conversion needed. We know we are summoned to a new way of living beyond the norms of the society we exist in. And we know that one decision to effect change will affect many structures and institutions as well as people in our society—a first step to repair social realities.

Repairing the world, *tikkun olam*—restoring wellness, health, wholeness—is our life's work, alone and with those in our communities. It is being called by God, in Jesus, to follow him: to come after him, to deny our very self, take up our cross, and walk in his footsteps (Matthew 16:24–25).

Jesus speaks, describing what life should look like: centering on restoring wholeness; and making sacred all things; and treating all others, especially the poor and those who have suffered most from violence, trauma, and rejection with a compassion that leads to repair.

Early in Mark's Gospel, Jesus tells a short parable as he is confronted by the Pharisees criticizing him and his disciples for not fasting in obedience with the traditional laws of Jewish spirituality. Jesus tells them there is a time for acting differently and doing something new. This parable is not one we hear often or pay much attention to, but it is fundamental, revealing how our lives must change to undo the harm we have done to others, and in participation with others.

> No one sews a patch of unshrunken cloth on an old cloak. If he should do so, the very thing he has used to cover the hole would pull away—the new from the old—and the tear would get worse. Similarly, no man pours new wine into old wineskins. If he does so, the wine will burst the skins and both wine and skins will be lost. No, new wine is poured into new skins. (Mark 2:21–22)

Jesus's prophetic words call us to new and radical ways of living in all areas of our lives and in how we relate to others. Even a short line like "love your enemies and do good to those who persecute you" (Matthew 5:43ff) shocks us and shakes us as we consider how thoroughly we must change our ways.

But Jesus's words about unshrunken cloths and old wineskins are not only prophetic but demanding action expressed in ordinary experiences. The Good News to the Poor is God's call to overhaul our lives and be converted to God's ways of living with each other. It's the call for enacting God's justice, with compassion and mercy, toward all. Jesus's words to us are fundamentally new, pushing beyond all the words of the prophets that came before him—not merely offering a commentary on how they are to be obeyed.

This parable speaks to how most of us react when we hear God's call and shows us what our lives are meant to look like. The parable reveals what we feel about those kinds of radical changes to our way of living.

When Jesus, the Word of God, became the flesh of the Father entering our human history, all that exists was created anew. The mystery of Incarnation is the mystery of the total transformation of all reality—beginning with what it means to be human. Here's how Martin Luther King Jr. preached about it in Montgomery, Alabama, in October 1954, at the Dexter Avenue Baptist Church.

> The long caravan of humanity had been moving in one direction for centuries, now it was to stop and change its course. Wherein it had been moving towards the city of legalism, it was now to move toward the city of Grace . . . . The new event which appeared in the coming of Jesus was so world shaking because it was contained in a new bottle of historical receptivity. Time and history were ready for his coming. . . . The real problem lies in the fact that this new fresh resolution is not coupled with a change in one general or overall structure of life. He has a new and fresh desire to change one segment of his life, but

this new desire is placed in the same old wornout general structure.

The old cloaks and all the structures and institutions of the world in history are now old wineskins. The coming of Jesus is a quantum shift in the evolution of humanity and the universe. But the newness must continue to happen over and over again—when there are periods in history that have deteriorated and the time comes for those realities to be undone.

We live in a time when this deterioration seems to be happening in many parts of the world simultaneously. Many Indigenous peoples and other cultural peoples were once enslaved, conquered, and brutalized, while other nations sought to assimilate them or exterminate them. They have risen—and continue to rise up, to claim their freedom, their dignity, and liberation to live in their *sacred manners* and traditional ways.

All the processes of repairing the world's structures and institutions among many peoples, nations, religions, even among men and women, children, and those aging are at a point in time where the sparks have been uncovered and discovered, and people are seeking to make holy people, relationships, places, and things that have been buried and hidden in the past. We find ourselves living in what seems often to be a time of continuing crises. In Asian societies and languages, the word for *crisis* is twofold. It is formed by two written characters that form a bridge or arch that a person or group must pass through. The two characters are translated as danger and possibility. Only by passing through the crisis do we know which one prevailed.

Many of Jesus's parables and teachings on how human beings function and survive in their societies deal with repairing the structures, existing conditions in institutions, and how society is sustained economically, socially, and religiously. And the parables clearly reveal how peoples create problems through injustice, inequality, enforced labor, poverty, and slavery that keep others and nations under existing forms of authority and power.

The Good News of God in Jesus's preaching has to make us aware of the universe, the earth, and all that constitutes how we dwell on this planet with other creatures, natural resources, and elements essential to our survival as the human race, the human community. This kind of awareness calls for us to practice *tikkun olam* in the immediate present and in planning for long-range actions, governing structures, laws, and philosophies that prioritize human thriving in existing institutions. *Tikkun olam* involves individual attitudes and communal values, ethics, and evolving, even radically altering ways of relating, communicating, and living in all areas of human life. It is the daunting task of religious practice, being a good human being, a good citizen, a good Christian (or believer related to one's religion), and living that goodness in relationship and community with others.

In the words of Leonard Peltier, a Native prophet, who has been imprisoned for decades, it is what we must make the cornerstone of our lives together: "Our voice, our collective voice, our eagle's cry, is just beginning to be heard. We call out to humanity. Hear us!" This cry is echoed by Oscar Romero in *Voice of the Voiceless*: when the church hears the pleas of the oppressed, it cannot but denounce the social structures that give rise to and perpetuate the misery from which the cry arises. And as the writer Terry Tempest Williams puts it in her essay "Unraveling," "We are Earth unraveling and reforming creation." However, to try to articulate the work of *tikkun olam* is a massive endeavor, a great challenge, and the task and gift that has been entrusted to all of us.

We begin by looking at the large picture and its horizons using one of Jesus's parables, found in Matthew's Gospel, called The Laborers in the Vineyard. It deals with many of the issues of repairing, reinvisioning, and creating new features of the structures we presently exist in as we understand the root causes of much harm that needs to be undone, repaired, and redesigned to make our lives holier, more whole.

The parable, like many of Jesus's stories, begins with the phrase: "The kingdom of God is like" (in other translations "the reign of God," or "the Kingdom of heaven") and then presents the situation that needs to be upset, overturned, along with the call to the conversion of people's hearts, attitudes, and ways of acting.

What does it mean? To look at the words *reign of God* in a different light, rather than reign as a political or legal hierarchical structure of kings and other authority figures, we might look at it as the *rein* of God—the words of Jesus that include the law and go beyond it, shifting the source toward the disciplines and forms that enable boundaries for growth and the evolution of human beings according to the Good News to the Poor.

The reins of God are held strongly in the hands of justice, compassion, and mercy, to be experienced equally by all. Or you could consider the *rain* of God. In many Indigenous and ancient societies, there are at least two major kinds of rain: male and female. Male rain primarily comes during the time called the rainy season, monsoons, with fierce storms, hurricanes, typhoons. They are characterized by their duration, the amount of rain, the side effects (flooding, wind, existing water surges, etc). They are hard rains meant to drive the seed into the ground during planting time, but they can also be destructive and cause widespread disasters. The female rain falls during other times of the year, when throughout the year there may be drought, long periods with lack of moisture, or lack of snow melt. It is much lighter rain, so light that sometimes, it doesn't even touch the ground, hanging in the air while it stills brings moisture and encourages plant growth; in warmer months, it cools the heated earth and air, providing relief.

The parables Jesus tells give us an experience of what it is like to become aware of living, dwelling, abiding in the presence of God everywhere, all ways, always. It is what life and existence are like as God's breath, God's blessing upon the earth as Jesus's beatitudes become reality among us in history, in the here and now. It's the way Jesus lives as a human being, as God made flesh among us, calling us to create our society, our world in the image of his original intent. "As it was, is, and will be, in the beginning," the Jewish community prays, referring to creation in Genesis.

This parable begins with the structure and institutions related to the functioning of one area of society in the case of the owner of the estate who "went out at dawn to hire workmen for his vineyard." The vineyard is the property of the owner, along with produce harvested on his land: in this instance, grapes. The owner employs workers to plant, water, weed, and harvest his grapes, and they are paid for their labor. There is an existing structure of payment based on hours of work in the fields—much the same as it is around the world where crops are raised by people, not machines.

We begin the story, meeting the groups of workers. The owner goes out to hire workers and makes a deal with them "an agreement for the usual daily wage," and sends the first hired group off to work. We learn further in the parable that the usual daily work hours begin at around dawn. Then he goes out again and hires a second group at midmorning. He hires new workers who have been waiting for work, and together they agree that he will pay them "whatever is fair." Off they go.

But the grapes need to be picked, and time is essential for the making of wine with fresh, fit grapes for distilling. So, the owner comes out again at noon and again at midafternoon for new hires. As the day progresses, he chooses others to go and work, probably with the same wage of the midmorning agreement: "whatever the owner decides is fair." And then with the day almost gone, and he's still in need of getting more of the grapes picked and brought in from the field, he goes out again in search for laborers. This time, he asks them "why they've been standing around idle all day and they tell him, no one hired us." The owner tells them, you, too, go along to the vineyard.

Now it is nearing evening, around 4 or 5 pm, and the owner calls in his foreman, telling him to assemble the workers all together and pay them, sending them home. But he adds a peculiar stipulation. "Begin with the last group and end with the first." And so, the foreman obeys the owner. Those hired last, who worked maybe an hour or so get paid, but they get paid a full day's wage! And so did all the others! Those who made the original agreement for the daily wage; those who took the arrangement for whatever was fair; and those who didn't make any deal, just went when they were told to go! Imagine what each person in each of the group was feeling and thinking!

Then the first group, who had worked all day, were made to wait on all the others who worked from around 9 am, then from noon, then around 3 pm, and those who barely did any work at all—seeing that the others all got a full day's wage. The first group wonders, what are we going to get—we worked more than all of them! But they get the same amount, which was their original negotiated payment. This group is angry, annoyed, put out. But they don't deal with the foreman, after getting their pay, they go to the top, to the owner himself, to complain. They tell him, we worked since sunup, and we bore the scorching heat of the day, and "you've put them, who didn't work as hard and long as we did on the same basis as us!" It is probably the foreman who probably accompanied them to meet with the owner at his house who hears their anger and reactions.

The owner addresses them as "my friends, I do you no injustice. You agreed on the usual wage, did you not? Take your pay and go home. I intend to give this man who was hired last the same pay as you. I am free to do as I please with my money, am I not? Or are you envious because I am generous?" (Matthew 20:9–15). None of them expected to be treated justly—as they arranged in the beginning—they compared themselves to all the others—and expected that if the others were treated justly, even though they didn't work the full day, the first group would get a better deal. The owner asks them if they are "envious" of what they consider the owner's generosity? But according to the foreman and the owner of this estate, the vineyard and Jesus's kin-dom reign (rain and rein), this *is* God's justice. And if this is God's justice, the way things should be for all, the way life should be for all, what then is God's generosity, God's restoration? What does God's repair of the world look like; what does God intend for life to look like?

It can help to consider how a vineyard operated at the time of Jesus (and often still does, with harvesting on large corporate-owned farms). Recalling the history of the farm worker movement in the last forty years, workers were hired at the crack of dawn, before the day's swelter, when it was easiest to pick and harvest—back-breaking and exhausting work. Those first picked (both men and women) were the strongest, in good health, and could keep picking as it got hotter and the day went on. The grapes needed to be picked on a tight schedule, so, the next group was still waiting to be chosen, but might be older, not as strong, or in good shape but could be expected to still work relatively hard for the rest of the day. At noon and at midafternoon, the labor pool became scarcer, and the remaining laborers were older men and women, those weaker, feebler, with disabilities, even troublemakers who caused dissension while working, and younger children. By the time the owner went out with maybe just an hour or less to work, it was those who had stood idle—not working all day since dawn, but not chosen because they were beggars, pregnant, sick, lame, outsiders, unable to work—those a foreman might consider near useless. It wasn't because they were lazy or refused to go to the vineyard but because they were the least, the poorest, and weren't desired in the fields by the owners or seen as equals by other workers. This helps us understand the last line of the parable a bit better. "Thus the last shall be first and the first shall be last."

In Jesus's world, in the world and society that Jesus came to bring to earth, this is what "Good News to the Poor" looks like when we are converted to imitate and be holy "as God is holy" with Jesus. The parables allow us to visit God's dream of what life can be like with grace and the Spirit. We are invited to catch a glimpse of the world restored, repaired, and re-created, and we are asked if we will be converted to making "life ever more abundant" for all, starting first with those who are the most traumatized, broken, persecuted, humiliated, excluded, abused, and shattered by violence and injustice.

If this parable is acted out in a group, in a circle beginning with the first group and then other groups arranged next to them and each other until all form a large circle with the last group's circle next to the first group's, everyone can see what Jesus is trying to tell them, and what the owner and foreman are trying to get them to understand in their relationship to others in the larger circle. Each group needs to be aware of the group on either side of them and what they are experiencing and in need of, and then realize that all must be treated equally, justly, with compassion and understanding, humanly, no matter who they are or what their situation in life might be.

When each group reacts, it has questions: If this is reality every day, what time are you going to show up for work tomorrow, and every day? How do you feel about the vineyard owner and foreman, and how do you feel about the people in the last group? If they share that among themselves in their small group first and then the foreman goes around the groups, starting with the last and has them share the answers to the questions in the large group, everyone learns something about Jesus's God as Father, Jesus as foreman.

All the people within the various groups learn how they need to change to act like Jesus. They learn how to be in relation with those who come first in God's care. It is difficult to listen to each of the groups, beginning with the last and making the earlier groups wait their turn to speak, but it gives a sense of what it is like to live at the bottom—to live as the "least"—as well as what needs to be converted: to do justice, to restore and to repair the structures, institutions, and systems so that people can live with dignity as they deserve to with their families and each other.

To repair structures, systems, and institutions, we must live a radically new way of life, in community with others, if we are to call ourselves Christians and those who are disciples and followers of Jesus. In a nutshell, as Curt Birchler posted on Facebook, "You cannot love your neighbor while supporting or accepting systems that crush, exploit and dehumanize others. You cannot love your neighbor while accepting less for them and their families than you do for your own." *Tikkun olam* is how we forgive, reconcile, do justice, and hold others responsible, restoring wholeness to those harmed, repairing our souls, relationships, and institutions, and living in communion, in harmony, and in peace together.

There is a marvelous process in Japan that describes what *tikkun olam* is like. It is called *kintsukuroi*, and for over five hundred years it has been considered an art form and a skill. It also has a simpler term, *kintsugi*, and is taught by masters, translated as "the art of golden repair." Developed in Japanese history, it's connected to the concept of *wabi-sabi*, which means to find beauty in ordinary things, especially in broken or old vessels.

It is easy to connect this art form to the reality of our broken lives and hearts. Whatever is broken is kept, and the pieces are put back together again with either liquid gold or silver lacquer. It is a painstakingly carefully executed process, time-consuming, with attention to detail and total concentration. A master holds classes, apprenticing those who wish to learn the discipline and art, which takes years to master. One learns about the lacquer, the materials of gold and silver, and the many different items that have been broken or aged: plates, tea cups, bowls, urns, vases, ritual objects. But the finished pieces are exquisite, often more sturdy, even more lovely when all their cracks, chips, holes, and broken spaces are exposed and can be seen!

We are all cracked deep in our hearts, souls, even minds and psyches, and we bear holes, scars, and broken places. And all can be repaired, restored, even made stronger and more whole, through the process of *tikkun olam*, or PTG, when we are attentive, careful of others, and tend to them in their search for healing, forgiveness, reconciliation, and restoration to wholeness, holiness and to becoming their true selves.

> *The eyes of the future are looking back at us and they are praying for us to see beyond our own time.*
>
> —Terry Tempest Williams

Into a daybreak that's wondrously clear I RISE, Bringing the gifts that my ancestors gave, I am the dream and the hope of the slave, I RISE, I RISE, I RISE.

—Maya Angelou

INTENTION, REFLECTION, RESPONSE

Let us not be so patient with other peoples' suffering. Never, never be afraid to do what's right, especially if the well-being of a person or an animal is at stake. Society's punishments are small compared to the wounds we inflict on our souls when we look the other way.

—Martin Luther King Jr.

Who lives close to you right now? Are their lives in need of transformation? Start with those in your church, your parish, your neighborhood, and become aware of them, so near you, yet, in reality, living in another world altogether? Who is different near you? Begin by praying to *see* the people around you and how they may be suffering. And then pray to participate in *tikkun olam*. Here's a simple prayer by Martin Luther King: "Use me, God. Show me how to take who I am, who I want to be, and what I can do, and use it for a purpose greater than myself."

> *We're not so much invited to declare our allegiance to a system of beliefs, but rather to a way of living, a way of loving—to a vision where we take seriously what Jesus took seriously—inclusion, non-violence, unconditional loving, kindness, and compassionate acceptance.*
>
> —Greg Boyle, SJ

If you're able to gather with a few other people, look together at one system you participate in daily that impacts money, time, other people who work in the system, those who control its operations, and either how it includes or excludes others through its rules and laws. Educate yourselves to understand how you either contribute to the problems it makes for others or how you can help the process better serve others' needs. And stay with it until together you find ways to make a difference and have agreed on how your group will implement those changes.

Martin Luther King Jr. made the blunt statement decades ago that "Our nation (the United States of America) was born in genocide when it embraced the doctrine that the original American, the Indian, was an inferior race." This is a history shared with other nations: Canada, the nations of Central and South America, Australia, New Zealand, and many countries of the world. It is our responsibility to work with Indigenous communities where we live and seek to mutually repair the effects and consequences of their experiences of forced separation, lost children, shattered families, boarding schools, poverty, imprisonment, abuse, disappearances, and problems that plague their communities today: suicide, alcoholism, health issues, trauma, violence, securing the basic necessities of survival, education—the litany of issues that need to be addressed is long. Consider educating yourself or your group with one or more of these resources:

- A Catholic Response to Call to Action 48 of the Truth and Reconciliation Commission, from the Canadian Conference of Catholic Bishops and others. You might choose to discuss and pray with each chapter.
- United Nations Declaration on the Rights of Indigenous Peoples.
- *Violence and Indigenous Communities: Confronting the Past and Engaging the Present*, Northwestern University Press, 2021.

How often do we hear or read about injustice, evil, trauma, and violence coming to light in recent years? Isn't it time to hear the truth and decide what the truth demands of us so the harm does not continue? So that, as the Gospel of Luke says, "the secrets will be uncovered, the truth will come forth, and God's thought about every behavior and action will be vindicated. What's done in the dark will come to light" (Luke 12:2–3). Are we reading to hear and learn the truth about the root cause of violence against different groups, such as Native women? Are we willing to allow the truth to penetrate the darkness? Is this part of our being the light we are longing for? (Adapted meditation from Indigenous Solidarity Collective Member, Mary Ann Reed.)

The Truth and Reconciliation Commission's Report, number 39 says, "We call upon the federal government to develop a national plan to collect and publish data on the criminal victimization of Aboriginal people, including data related to homicide and family violence victimization."

As an individual or with a group, pick a people group and learn about their struggle to heal, be restored to wellness, and live with justice.

There is a simple First Nations' story. I call it Hermit Crab's Home. It speaks of how we are to live, repairing the many aspects of the world: our lives, bodies, and souls; our relationships; our societies and systems. A small girl and boy were sitting on the steps of their front porch. The house was almost empty, as all the members of the family had spent most of the morning carrying out all their belongings, furniture, clothes, cooking utensils, and treasures. They had gone through the empty rooms and now sat, almost in tears, knowing it was time to leave for good. They all sat together before leaving, all feeling the loss and the pain of having to start over again. But then one of the older ones remembered something his grandmother had told them.

Do you remember when we'd all go crabbing on the beach? We saw some of the crabs that live in shells crawl out of the one they were in, and they headed for another one, bigger. We learned they were hermit crabs, and they would regularly grow too big for the shell they were in. They'd find another one and when it was time, squirm and wiggle out of their old one, and when they found a bigger home, they'd move in. And they'd start to carry their new home around like the old one. They'd leave the old empty ones on the sand—maybe another hermit crab needed their old one.

They sat quietly for a while. Mother said—we've outgrown this house and need more space so we can keep living together. When we move, we can arrange our things the way we want them, so we feel more at home, and there will be space for other things, even more people to live with us. We'll make it our home. Besides, who lives in the house is what makes it a home, not our stuff, or even the space and what we've gotten used to.

If we don't move now, when we need to, our lives will just get more difficult. Grandfather said often that we need to keep changing, moving out of our old shells so we can grow, learn new things, tell new stories, and know each other better. It's time; let's go live our new lives together.

We live, repairing and restoring our lives together. And we are called to keep remembering.

"My humanity is bound up in yours for we can only be human together," Desmond Tutu once said. And we keep being reborn, re-created, being made new, changing, transforming, and being transformed, learning to live resurrection life now, as practice for "forever."

Afterword

We Rise Together

There will come a time when you believe everything is finished. That will be the beginning.

—Anonymous

We have only just begun
to imagine the fullness of life.
How could we tire of hope?
—so much is in bud.

—Denise Levertov

Make ready for the Christ, whose smile, like lightning,
sets free the song of everlasting glory that now sleeps,
in your paper flesh, like dynamite.

—Thomas Merton

Forgiveness sets the mystery of resurrection in motion. But what exactly is resurrection? If we first look at resurrection in theological terms, there are three main beliefs in Christianity:

1. That God the Father raised Jesus from the dead in the power of the Spirit and that Jesus is more alive now than when he walked the earth.
2. That God the Father will raise us—resurrect us—from the dead, with Jesus, in the power of the Spirit and that we, too, will know life more fully graced, more alive, than when we lived on earth.
3. That resurrection begins at baptism, with incorporation and initiation into the risen Body of Christ's presence and power on earth and that the rest of our lives as believers is practice for the fullness of resurrection.

In many ways, the last statement is the one that impacts us most strongly and immediately. The mystery and gift of resurrection life is given to us over and over again, with every experience of being forgiven, reconciled with others and with God, blessed by God (often through others' connections to us), and ritually in the sacrament of baptism. But there has always been baptism by desire—take the desire to belong to God, even if it's not formalized in a religious ritual like water baptism. But it happens when we forgive: we raise people from the deadness of their lives, snatch them back from despair and isolation that kills souls and spirits. And it happens when we are forgiven as we experience the brush of resurrection, like the breath of the Spirit on our souls, our bodies, and in our lives.

Because God our Father raised Jesus, giving him back existence and life eternal, the reality, the power, and the presence of resurrection have been seeded and seep through the whole world, out into the whole universe. One of the strongest ways to experience it is through the gift of forgiveness, which blooms into reciprocal, mutual forgiving that is reconciliation and is completed by restoring justice, wholeness, and holiness to once-broken areas of our lives and relationships.

We are set free from what dies in us, what is torn from us, what harms ourselves, others, and our connections with God. In that freedom, we experience a moment, a taste of what it means to be made in God's image, to be created as the beloved children of God, drawn close as his friends, bound more deeply than any kinship by blood, or other ritual relationship.

Even hearing a story about forgiveness has the power to set us free, to lift us in hope and raise our spirits, our hearts and souls once again, to draw us into the power of resurrection. This is an old Jewish story, originally told by the Baal Shem Tov (which means the Master of the Good Name), the founder of the mystical tradition of the Hasidism started in Ukraine and that moved through Eastern Europe. He lived, preached, and taught joy, relief from the worst of human miseries, release from suffering, the sense of deep inner peace, the redemption of people from despair, and the setting of them on the path of undoing any harm that they had experienced or done to others.

Once upon a time there was a man who made his way through life telling stories. He had heard of the Besht (a shortened version of the Baal Shem Tov many referred to him by) and of the stories he told. The man journeyed and met the Besht, wanting to learn to tell tales like he did—that set people free, blessing their lives for the future.

The man was invited to stay with him for six months, to listen and learn. The Besht told him, watch me closely, see what I do, and who comes to see me. You'll have enough tales to tell for the rest of your life, and with practice, perhaps you too will use your stories to relieve others' pain and sorrow.

After the six months observing the Besht, the man was off to his new life, but he soon found that most people didn't even want to listen to his stories. His life was hard; there were few places or people who wanted to hear his tales, except sometimes in taverns, at markets, or on the street. He was often so discouraged.

One night he'd been at an inn, and even there no one was interested or wanted to listen to him. Finally, the innkeeper spoke to him: "Look, I know nobody here is interested, but I do know someone who definitely will listen to your stories. He's a Polish nobleman, incredibly wealthy, and he pays good money for every story he's told, that he hasn't heard before."

The man was given directions by the innkeeper and set off on the cold snowy night to find the man's great house. It was well lighted, and guarded, and he was ushered in to the great room. He was questioned about the purpose of his visit. He answered simply: "I have a story to tell." He was then taken to another room, where the nobleman was seated at a long table, with a pile of kopecks in front of him. The wandering storyteller was seated at the other end of the table. And he started telling stories, but the nobleman barely reacted. He nodded once in a while, and more rarely, he shoved a kopeck or two down the table when a story was told he hadn't heard before.

Finally, the poor man ran out of stories. He got up to leave, but the rich man asked him, "Is that all? You don't have anymore?" The teller hesitated.

"Uh, yes there is one more story," he says. "Once, when I was staying with the Baal Shem Tov, the man I learned many of my stories from, someone came to him utterly distraught, upset, in despair. He told him that once he had been a Jew, but gave up his practices, went out and made money, hungry for everything in the world. He did whatever he wanted, even stealing from others, beggaring the poor and harming many to make his fortune."

"He told the Besht, 'I even became a Christian and am highly esteemed in the towns where I travel and work. But I'm miserable. I did so many wrong things, treated people so badly, did evil—what should I do? How do I escape what I've become, what I've done?'

"The Besht comforted him, and said, 'Have no fear. From now on just help the poorest, share all you have with those in need, do justice, and use all you've learned to care for the least who are around you.'

"He agreed and promised he would do so immediately, but he was still so miserable. He asked again and again, 'when will I know that I've been forgiven?'

"Surprisingly, the Besht told the man, 'When you hear this story told to you one day in the future, you'll know you're forgiven and your life is being blessed. You are free. Live in peace.' "

At these words, the man at the other end of the table looked up. Then he rose, standing up, he began to walk down toward the storyteller. His face was radiant and there was a lightness to his step. He began to weep and embraced the storyteller, whispering, "you have set me free!"

It is said, that for every one of us, there is at least one person, for some there are many other human beings, who wait for those words of forgiveness, a story of hope, of justice, and of reconciliation, and that every one of us is the person all the others wait for. And when that moment comes, when they meet, both know that history has changed and both lives are redeemed and transformed forever. The mystery of our lives is that we live to give forgiveness, freedom, and the fullness of life to others.

It is our privilege to listen to others' stories and to tell our own—how we are forgiven, reconciled, learn the art of restoration, do justice, have our lives repaired in some way, and use our knowledge and experience to repair the world and all those around us. This is resurrection.

The gospel, the Good News of God to the Poor is God's

story in Jesus shared with us to give away to others, as we seek to return the favor of our lives, of being forgiven and being made holy over and over again.

The poet Maya Angelou reminds us that "there is no greater agony than bearing an untold story inside you."

And the Nigerian poet and author, Chinua Achebe writes in *Things Fall Apart*: "It is the storyteller who makes us what we are, who creates history. The storyteller creates the memory that the survivors must have—otherwise their surviving would have no meaning." Once we have been freed, and forgiven, we live to set others free and to forgive others, to invite them to tell their stories and add their stories to the story of the Resurrection of Jesus.

One of the earliest gospel stories of the resurrection is found in Mark, written about thirty to forty years after Jesus's life, death, and resurrection, and told by word of mouth, shared with everyone, before it was written down in the account we now share in the gospel. It is disarmingly short and to the point.

> When the Sabbath was over, Mary Magdalene, Mary the mother of James, and Salome brought perfumed oils with which they intended to go and anoint Jesus. Very early, just after sunrise, on the first day of the week they came to the tomb. They were saying to one another, "Who will roll back the stone for us from the entrance to the tomb?" When they looked, they found that the stone had been rolled back; it was very large.

The scene is first set with several details. They have stayed together after Jesus's burial and celebrated the Sabbath together—the group of disciples, followers, and friends of Jesus. Part of the ritual of the Sabbath meant not speaking of death while remembering the great deeds God had done for his people in liberating them from slavery and bondage, but rather singing and praying the psalms, blessing God.

So, the ones who gather wait together but do not speak of Jesus's suffering, death, and burial. They wait until the Sabbath is finished. We are told it is still dark, early in the morning, just after the sun has risen, with lingering night shadows and the chill air of first light.

Though we know from other accounts that at least eight others came to the tomb, the three women named are Mary of Magdala; Mary, the mother of James (thought to be the *other* James of the twelve disciples, sometimes called James the Lesser); and Salome, believed to be the woman who, in an earlier chapter in Mark anoints Jesus, who tells her she was anointing him for burial and that what she has done will be told of her wherever the gospel is proclaimed (14:3–9).

As the women come to the tomb, they bring the necessary burial oils, wrapping cloths, and a *shroud* (the same word used to describe him wrapped in swaddling cloth and laid in the manger when he was an infant). In all, the materials would have weighed about ninety pounds, and they now carried them to the tomb to minister to the body, offering what was considered one of the strongest acts of mercy, especially if the dead person was a convicted criminal. Just offering this corporal work of mercy made them unclean.

As they head to the tomb, all they can talk about is how they are actually going to get *into* the tomb. It is a small burial cave hewn out of rock, and sealed with a large stone, the size of a boulder.

Who is going to open the tomb so that they can get in? They're attempting to do what seems impossible–going to a tomb when they didn't know how they would move the stone–but they are desperate to get to Jesus's body, which was hastily put in the tomb before the sun went down that Friday, marking the beginning of the Sabbath. As they came to the tomb, they were shocked to find the tomb wide open.

> On entering the tomb, they saw a young man sitting at the right, dressed in a white robe and they were utterly amazed. He said to them: "Do not be amazed! I know you seek Jesus of Nazareth, the crucified. He has been raised; he is not here. Behold, the place where they laid him. But go and tell his disciples and Peter, "He is going before you to Galilee; there you will see him, as he told you." Then they went out and fled from the tomb, seized with trembling and bewilderment. They said nothing to anyone, for they were afraid. (Mark 16:7–8)

They are shocked to see the young man sitting off to the right of where the body would be, dressed in a white garment. Some translations changed the wording to say *an angel*, but it is a young man. Traditionally the four gospel writers put themselves in each of their gospels as people who believe and proclaim Jesus as Lord.

Here the young man is traditionally held to be Mark. We last saw him in the garden when Jesus is betrayed and arrested. He runs away, as the soldiers try to grab him, and he loses his garment, running naked into the night. But in the tomb, he is now clothed in a white robe, a baptismal garment, standing fast and proclaiming Jesus risen from the dead. In all the gospels, the act of entering the tomb and seeking the Lord, is to be baptized. As all the women disciples who sought to honor Jesus's body entered the tomb, they were *baptized*, drawn into the Body of Christ and told to now share his resurrection.

They are startled, confused, terrified. "Deeply disturbed" is the wording in one of the earlier translations, a phrase that appears a number of times in the gospels to signify that something traumatic, catastrophic is happening, which will affect everyone, shifting history from this moment. The young man speaks to them: "Do not be afraid," a more descriptive word than *amazed*. "I know you are looking, seeking, Jesus of Nazareth, the crucified one. He has been raised. He is not here."

This is the fundamental statement of Mark's community about who Jesus is: the man from Nazareth, crucified and now the Risen One, not to be found in any tomb, not *here*. They are instructed to see where he was laid and then to GO! He's not here, where you look for him. He's not in any tomb. He's not to be found in a garden burial ground, on the edge of the city of Jerusalem, the city of the ancients, where all the prophets are killed. The women are told to go to Galilee where they would find him. Galilee, in the north, is where the disciples first started out as Jesus left Nazareth and went to Jerusalem, preaching the Good News of God along the way. When the man speaks from the tomb, he's basically telling them to go back home. Go back to their beginnings.

The young messenger is very specific: Go now and tell his disciples and Peter. He's going ahead of you to Galilee, where you will see him, just as he told you. Go and proclaim his life, his presence, his words—to the disciples—and to Peter. These words are devastating in their own way. Peter is with the others, but he is no longer considered *a disciple*. Earlier he betrayed Jesus, staunchly refused to even admit he knew Jesus, refusing to stand with him or be associated with him in any way. He is not one of them at the moment.

Part of the resurrection stories that continue after this first installment will tell of how Peter repented, was forgiven, and reconciled to the others in the community and to Jesus himself, but according to the synoptic gospels, entrance into the tomb is a clear profession of belief in Jesus, and Peter does not enter the tomb.

The women are instructed to return back and go north to Galilee—about ninety miles. Galilee is bordered by other countries, all gentiles, unbelievers, even described as a place *where nothing good comes from*. And we are told that those who came to the tomb, obey.

They bolt. They flee from the tomb, *bewildered*, terrified, confused, and afraid. And in their fear, they remained silent, saying nothing to the other disciples. In the original ending of Mark's Gospel, this is the story that closes the book. The rest of the text that we know today was added on, here and there, because many didn't know what to do with this blunt, truncated ending so abrupt and disconcerting.

The women say nothing to *anyone*. It's crucial we know who is meant by anyone. Yet we know they obey, and they tell the disciples and those gathered around Jesus when he came into the city for the Passover. And we know they go back to Galilee together.

"Anyone" was thought to be about seventy to ninety people, families, children, the disciples, and other followers of Jesus, traveling caravan-style back home. And they must have talked to each other all the way. They told their stories of Jesus and encountering him, his effect on them, sharing their conversions, their beliefs, and who he is to them now. And they shared their *resurrection* stories—of empty tombs, running back and forth, no body, and what they had been told—that they'd see him again there in Galilee.

This is resurrection—at least three women (and as many as five more in other accounts) intent on doing a corporal work of mercy, in impossible circumstances, putting themselves in jeopardy knowing consequences of their actions will cause them to be shunned and penalized. And in the process of doing a work of mercy, they walk right into the face of death and run into resurrection—God with us, Jesus raised from the dead, and all of us created to live in the power and presence of God who dwells in us now sharing his resurrection, his intention that we be holy, that we become whole and full of grace, to live with God, like the way God lives now in us.

The Gospel of Mark is written as a circle, or a spiral that keeps repeating and coming back again and again upon itself. It begins with John the Baptist going before the Lord to prepare his way. John's preaching follows the tradition of another prophet: Isaiah. The first words are: "Here begins the gospel of Jesus Christ, the Son of God."

They return to hear and preach the Word of God again. And every time we read the gospel and seek to live the Good News of God to the Poor, we go back and start over yet again. Rereading the words, sharing our stories, and seeking Jesus of Nazareth, who we now know is prophet and more, beloved of God, preacher, Word made flesh, crucified and risen, now living among us *here*, everywhere, alive and with us for all time.

They go *home* and, on the way, they become not only disciples of Jesus but his friends, his community, and the church together. This is the way it is meant to be with us: together becoming the beloved children of God, walking each other home with the Risen Jesus, becoming those who live in freedom, holy and pleasing to God, friends with one another and with God.

Each of us has our resurrection story that starts after our death, our conversion to life and hope, our coming together again, our being touched by God's Spirit and re-created and made new. Willie James Jennings in his book *Acts: A Theological Commentary on the Bible*, puts it this way: "We who follow Jesus are working with wounds, and working through wounds."

Each of us begins the journey back to wholeness, to life ever more abundant, to what can be by grace and God's Spirit in sharing our stories with one another, adding our story to that of Jesus of Nazareth, crucified and now risen and alive in us, with us. Sharing our stories, sharing our lives through the gospel, with others, strengthens us and gives us solidarity with others to continue our journeys to liberation and fullness of life.

We learn from one another, sharing knowledge, wisdom, and our own experiences so that each of us can grow, mature, and become more human. And we can learn from anyone, anywhere, even from very unlikely sources, people, and cultures. Everyone has resurrection accounts and experiences, of coming back to life, uncovering depth, integrity, and sheer fullness of hope and joy to share with others. Here is a fairly recent story from First Nations' traditions.

Once upon a time, a wolf came out of her den, with her new litter trailing along behind her, stumbling, falling over each other, getting used to their new legs and a world they'd never seen before. Their eyes were getting used to leaving the dark, their noses twitched with fresh air and their feet were trying to keep their balance as they touched ground that was wet, covered with ruts, rocks, and all sorts of things they sniffed and even tried to chew on.

Over the next days and weeks, they learned about their new home that stretched for miles, where to find water, and where to rest and sleep and to watch out for other things they were meeting and what might be dangerous. And they were learning how to find things to eat, too. And so one day it was time to learn how to catch fish! They came to the river, fast flowing waters, and plunged in, getting used to splashing, and looking for fish to catch. There were a lot of them, but they were fast and hard to catch.

Wolf mother tried hard biting at one, then another. Finally, after a good long while, she caught a small one, took it to the bank where they gathered around, and she plopped down gasping for air from the strain of trying to catch one. Then each pup chewed a little on the small fish.

"Now," she said, "It's your turn; go catch one for yourself."

In they went, pushing and shoving, grabbing at anything that went by them—fast, slithering away from them, even sliding out of their paws and mouths. They tired easily. Finally, one pup just stopped, exhausted, standing still in the water, having a drink and trying to breathe. He was very still, catching his breath. Just then a big fish who didn't notice him swam right up near him, thinking he was a rock, and the wolf pup moved fast, and grabbed him, got him good. He brought it over to his mother wolf and laid it down saying, "Look! I caught this one by just stopping and doing nothing and it just came right up to me! I'm going to do it my way, instead of yours, running all over and trying to grab them."

The older wolf said, "That's not the way to do it. You need to learn my way, like I learned from my mother and she from hers. It's tried and true."

While she was correcting him, another of the pups had seen what his sister wolf had done, and imitated her, and caught another big one, just like she had done, by just standing still and waiting for a fish to come near. Soon, in spite of their mother's lesson, all the young ones were bringing back big fish and having a feast. The older wolf was not pleased and stood on the bank, barking at them to do it the *right* way, her way.

An eagle was flying overhead, watching and laughing, and swooped down near the bigger wolf. "Look, mother, it seems like your young ones can teach you something instead of you being the teacher all the time. Admit it—their way is better, easier, and doesn't wear them out so much."

Finally, the mother wolf agreed "You're right. Their way is much better—and off she went to try it herself."

And the eagle who often saw things from another angle altogether yelled out, "It's good to learn from others, and to be willing to change." Parents and elders can even learn from their children, or strangers—just because you've done it this way all the time doesn't mean it's the only way, or even the best way. Everyone has their own wisdom and experience, and we can learn from the least likely animals, our own kind, and all creatures and things.

On our journeys to wholeness, to healing, and restoring our lives, we can learn from everyone. Our differences feed our creativity, bridge the gaps between us, and form us anew, affirming others' knowledge and ways of living, helping us to live in community. Our differences can become our strengths that tie and bind us more closely together. In fact, many small resurrections that we need are found in our differences and in what seem to separate us from each other.

A South African teacher shared with me what some of their people have learned. "Ubuntu is about reaching out to our fellow men and women, through whom we might just find the comfort, contentment and sense of belonging we crave. Ubuntu tells us that individuals are nothing without other human beings. It encompasses everyone, regardless of race, creed or color. It embraces our differences and celebrates them."

Or, as one Diné woman, quoting Black Elk to me, said, "Grown men and women may learn from very little children, for the hearts of little children are pure, and therefore, the Great Spirit may show to them many things which older people miss."

It is not only children who can teach those of us who are older. Perhaps our greatest teachers are those who have suffered physically and who in their *difference* from others, in their grief, poverty, and the pain of exclusion, teach us through their seeking to connect, their openness with others.

In fact, all those we meet are the *blessed* of Jesus's friends, who teach just by their presence in our lives. The poor, those who sorrow, the lowly, and those who hunger and thirst still for justice teach us how to yet show mercy: all those who are single-heartedly devoted to life, forgiveness, integrity, and truth; all those who make peace, build bridges, and open pathways and doors for those *outside* us; all those who have known persecution, humiliation, shunning, and physical abuse who still seek life, live in hope, and share their joy are our teachers, the ones who teach us most. They are living, breathing sighs, and songs of resurrection among us. They are the ones who know God most deeply and live to share that wisdom with others but especially those most desperate for life, for inclusion, for hospitality and our expression of love.

There is an old story that tells of how we live in a death-defying way that speaks of how to live resurrection, sharing life with others. It is from the Maumee tradition (northern Wisconsin). Once upon a time, the Great Spirit made all the animals and gave them their freedom, putting them on earth—Turtle Island—where they roamed freely. All went well for a while, and then Eagle got bored. He decided to challenge the other animals to a race, and whoever would win would enslave the other. First, he went after the bear and beat him easily, as the bear was coming out of hibernation and was slow. Then it was hawk, osprey, and then, one by one, all the other animals until practically all of them were slaves of Eagle. Pretty soon, Turtle and Muskrat, who were good friends, were the only ones who remained free. They lived off by themselves near a pond and hid there a lot.

One day Turtle awoke and told his friend Muskrat that the Great Spirit had come to him in a dream and told him to challenge Eagle to a race! Muskrat thought that it was a good idea that the Great Spirit came to his friend in a dream but not that he was to challenge Eagle to race.

Muskrat asked him, "Did he [Great Spirit] tell you how to beat him?"

Turtle answered him, "No, he didn't. You will have to find out with the others." So off they went.

Eagle was surprised to see them (he knew there were a couple of holdouts), but he listened and said, "Okay, we'll race."

Then Turtle said, "But now we will change the stakes—whoever wins this one will be special—if I win, I set all the animals free and if you win, then you will have everyone as your slaves."

"Okay," said Eagle.

"And if I, the Turtle beat you, the Eagle, I get to tell the story and then everyone can tell the story too!

Eagle looked at Turtle and had a good laugh: "Okay," he said, knowing he'd win for sure.

Word got around fast that there was going to be another race—the one that could set all of them free. Expectations and hopes rose, until someone realized and reminded them that Turtle couldn't even beat a snail, let alone Eagle. But they all decided to root for Turtle because he was their only hope.

Next morning they all showed up. Eagle was feeling good, and said, "You can decide where the race begins and ends."

"Oh, thank you," said Turtle, relieved. "I know exactly where it begins. You pick me up and carry me in your talons as high as you can and then drop me—and whoever hits the ground first wins!"

Eagle looked at him surprised, but there was no way he could back out now.

So, he grabbed ahold of him and up and up they went, with Turtle in Eagle's claws, and then Turtle yelled out "DROP ME!" and the race was on. They were close, side by side. Turtle falling like a rock and Eagle streaking like an arrow—neck and neck while all the animals cheered loudly. Then Muskrat thought to himself—if Turtle beats Eagle, he's going to die or be hurt terribly. I don't know if my friend's life is worth our freedom. But the race was almost over. At the last minute, Eagle surged ahead and then swooped away from the ground. Turtle hit the ground hard.

All the animals gathered around quietly. Turtle didn't move for a long, long time. Finally, one foot came out, then another, and finally his head, spinning around. They all cheered.

They were all free to roam again—anywhere they wanted, and to tell the story of how Turtle beat Eagle!

Soon there was no one left but Eagle and Turtle and Muskrat together. Eagle asked him "How did you know how to beat me? You didn't get that on your own, even if you are wise."

"You're right," Turtle said. "The Great Spirit came to me in a dream and told me to challenge you and how to beat you. However, he didn't tell me that I'd live—only that I'd set the animals free. And he told me other things: that soon, two-leggeds will come to this place Turtle Island. They will be red and they will follow me, and they will listen to the dreams of the Great Spirit.

"They will always be free in this land. Then later, much much later, other two-leggeds will come from across the great waters. They will be white and they will follow the eagle, but they will not listen to the dreams of the Great Spirit and they will not be free even if they try. Remember, Eagle, that you are not all powerful and that the Great Spirit wants us all to live in freedom on all the lands that were created."

In many creation stories from Indigenous peoples that seek to describe why things are the way they are today, probably the most important detail of how to win and set people free is the risk: "The Great Spirit told me how to set them free, but the Great Spirit didn't tell me that I'd live." We are here to forgive one another as we have been forgiven and now live in the freedom of God's beloved community of friends. Once we are forgiven and free, we are to set others free and share this gift of living, as the Great Spirit has created us to be with each other, all others.

In the gospels we read, as though we were overhearing, one of Jesus's prayers, "Yes, Father, you have graciously willed it so. Everything has been given over to me by my Father. No one knows the Son except the Father and no one knows the Father except the Son—and anyone to whom the Son wishes to reveal him" (Luke 10:21c–22). "Anyone" Jesus reveals God to—anyone who has known forgiveness and the Good News of being the beloved ones that God treasures, is baptized into the resurrection. Once we know forgiveness, we are drawn closer to God, and drawn deeper into their communion as Three, yet One. We know more of home and what it was that we have been created for—intimacy, freedom, and holiness with one another and God.

We were born to reveal God and to live with God, *like* God. Amazing! A marvelous short story by Rabbi Wolpe is an apt close to this chapter and this book. Once upon a time a man or a woman once stood before God; their hearts were breaking from their pain and the injustice in the world. They cried out, "Dear God, look at all the suffering, the anguish and distress in your world. Why don't you send help?"

God responded, "I did send help. I sent you!"

When we tell this story to our children, we must tell them that each one of them was sent to help repair the broken world—and that it is not the task of an instant or of a year, but of a lifetime.

We must live in such a way that we are reaching out to touch others with each breath, each gesture, each work. "Every breath we draw is a gift . . . every moment of existence is a grace," wrote Thomas Merton. We are all home here on this earth, we are all going home together. We all fall and rise together. God is with us. All of us are alive and live with grace in God. Go! Go, and you will see him, just as he told you. Go. Go with God.

INTENTION, REFLECTION, RESPONSE

> *What we hunger for perhaps more than anything else is to be known in our full humanness, and yet that is often just what we also fear more than anything else. It is important to tell at least from time to time the secret of who we truly and fully are . . . because otherwise we run the risk of losing track of who we truly and fully are and little by little come to accept instead the highly edited version which we put forth in hope that the world will find it more acceptable than the real thing. It is important to tell our secrets because it makes it easier . . . for other people to tell us a secret or two of their own.*
>
> —Frederick Buechner

Take some time to gather your *secrets* together, in writing, or pictures or symbols. Then spend some time looking around: who would you like to tell one secret to? Start a conversation, that can become a *communion* of your spirits together.

Walking I am listening to a deeper way. Suddenly all my ancestors are behind me. Be still, they say. Watch and listen. You are the result of the love of thousands.

—Linda Hogan

Make a litany of your ancestors. But not just ones intimately connected to you through blood or marriage. Who is connected to you through support, faith, holiness, and wisdom shared—those in many traditions we refer to as *saints* or *holy ones*. Remember their struggles and the sparks they bent over and breathed on, stirring them into flame. How have they stirred flame for you? How are they still impacting your changes, development, and becoming all fire?

The marks life leaves on everything it touches transform perfection into wholeness. Older, wiser cultures choose to claim this wholeness in the things they create. In Japan, Zen gardeners choose purposefully to leave a fat dandelion in the midst of the exquisite, ritually precise patterns of the meditation garden. In Iran, even the most skilled of rug weavers includes an intentional error, the "Persian Flaw," in the magnificence of a Tabriz or Qashqai carpet . . . and Native Americans wove a broken bead, the "spirit bead" into every beaded masterpiece. Nothing that has a soul is perfect. When life weaves a spirit bead into your very fabric, you may stumble upon a wholeness greater than you had dreamed possible before.

—Rachel Naomi Remen

In reflecting upon your life, what sparks—or marks—have been woven into your life that transform and alter everything you do, your relationships, your work? When you know what it is, what can you do to make it a piece of beauty, a streak of sacredness that adds something of grace to your life, making it more whole than you previously thought possible?

Resurrection is laced into every aspect of our lives. Recall the meaning of the word *resurrection* is "to stand up." All the practices of resurrection, as a way of life, as moral and ethical stances and as spiritual ways are based on standing up. Each practice is based on God the Father and the Spirit standing up for Jesus in his life and our God who is Three, in the Trinity standing up for us as we stand for what Jesus preached and practiced in his life and shared with us in the gospel.

Below are ten practices to use and to share with others to experience resurrection now, here, together.

- TO STAND UP FOR—as in a court of law, to witness to, in public to align oneself with, as a character witness. God the Father and the Spirit witnessed to Jesus in this sense in John's Gospel. We attest to the integrity and truthfulness of others and their actions with them.
- TO STAND BEHIND—it was an understanding of the early church that God the Father stood behind Jesus as he *fell* in death on the cross. As he fell, the Father caught him and stood him back up again and breathed the Spirit's life—their life—into him again. Stand behind others, saying, "I've got your back," even if your back is up against a wall for support. We do this for others, and God does it for us.

- TO STAND IN SOLIDARITY WITH—to stand in solidarity is to physically put your body next to or with others' bodies, in place and space. This can entail what some clergy and teachers call pushing your privilege in society, with your connections. You put your body there, literally *there* with them.
- TO STAND IN COMMUNION WITH—is a more difficult challenge in a sense. It is putting everything at the disposal and service of others—prayer, energy, money, support, resources, etc. Think of going to communion—as intimate and close as the reception of the Eucharist is what it means to be in communion totally with others as they need.
- TO STAND AGAINST—is a prophetic stance, against all death, evil, violence, sin, injustice, trauma. To be death-defying as Jesus was—and as life-affirming.
- TO STAND IN FOR—is giving up one's life for another—martyrdom in its original sense, to give your life so another might live. But more often it is more mundane and daily—as in 24/7 caregiving for others so that they may have life, ever more abundantly now, rather than just survive.
- TO STAND DOWN—this is the stance of always forgiving, everyone, all the time. It is the fourfold process of being forgiving of others

    - to forgo all revenge, getting even, and making others pay;
    - to forbear your share of the burden of the gospel and bear all wrongs patiently, knowing when to just *let it go* and when to stand with others;
    - to forget, to make new memories so that the next time you see or hear a person, you do not immediately revert to that incident;

  - to forgive, which often begins with praying for those who have harmed you, asking God to help you forgive and praying for their conversion and your own, along with grace for you and for them.

- TO STAND ASIDE—to give others the credit or acclaim, honor, or glory. To do things anonymously, generously, or for the good of the group. To learn to *disappear* and do good as God does, without expecting to be noticed or praised.
- TO STAND TOGETHER—while any of these practices may be done as an individual, one of the foundations of our faith is that God is a Trinity, a community, and so, anything we do together witnesses and reveals the communal nature of our God. Together there is power and strength, imagination and creativity, beyond anything one person can do.
- TO STAND FAST—is faithfulness, enduring with grace, and, in the words of Daniel Berrigan, to "hang on for a dearer life." It is a presence that is based on the bedrock of the resurrection despite and through all that happens and when nothing seems to be changing and all seems lost.

Mitakuye oyasin—all my relations—
May we all be one, in God, as God is Three, in One.

For Further Reading

Arendt, Hannah. *The Human Condition*. 2nd ed. Chicago: University of Chicago Press, 1998.

Baldwin, James. *James Baldwin: The Complete Works*. New York: BN Publishing, 1972.

——. *Notes of a Native Son*. Boston: Beacon Press, 2012.

——. *The Fire Next Time*. New York: Vintage International, 2013.

——. *Go Tell It on the Mountain*. New York: Vintage International, 2013.

——. *Nothing Personal*. Boston: Beacon Press, 2021.

Baum, Gregory. *The Oil Has Not Run Dry: The Story of My Theological Pathway*. Montreal: McGill-Queen's University Press, 2018.

Berrigan, Daniel. *To Dwell in Peace: An Autobiography*. New York: HarperCollins, 1987.

——. *Wisdom: The Feminine Face of God*. Chicago: Sheed & Ward, 2001.

——. *Sorrow Built a Bridge: Friendship and AIDS*. Eugene, OR: Wipf and Stock, 2009.

——. *Testimony: The Word Made Flesh*. Maryknoll, NY: Orbis, 2004.

——. *The Dark Night of Resistance.* Eugene, OR: Wipf and Stock, 2007.

Black Elk. *The Sacred Pipe: Black Elk's Account of the Seven Rites of the Oglala Sioux.* Norman, OK: University of Oklahoma Press, 1989.

——. *Sacred Ways of a Lakota.* New York: HarperCollins Publishers, 1991.

Boyle, Greg, SJ. *Tattoos on the Heart: The Power of Boundless Compassion.* New York: Free Press, 2011.

——. *Barking to the Choir: The Power of Radical Kinship.* New York: Simon & Schuster Paperbacks, 2017.

——. "Foreword," in Thomas Vozzo, *The Homeboy Way: A Radical Approach to Business and Life.* Chicago: Loyola Press, 2022.

Buber, Martin. *Tales of the Hasidim.* New York: Schocken Books, 1991.

——. *Between Man and Man.* New York: Routledge, 2002.

——. *I and Thou.* New York: Free Press, 2023.

Buechner, Frederick. *Telling Secrets.* New York: HarperOne, 2000.

Burger, Ariel. *Witness: Lessons from Elie Wiesel's Classroom.* Boston: Houghton Mifflin Harcourt, 2018.

Cantacuzino, Marina. *The Forgiveness Project: Stories for a Vengeful Age.* London: Jessica Kingsley Publishers, 2016.

Casaldáliga, Pedro, *In Pursuit of the Kingdom: Writings, 1968–1988.* Maryknoll, NY: Orbis Books, 1990.

Casaldáliga, Pedro, and José María Vigil. *Political Holiness: A Spirituality of Liberation.* (Theology and Liberation), Maryknoll, NY: 1994.

Catherine of Sienna, Saint. *The Dialogue of St. Catherine of Siena: A Conversation with God on Living Your Spiritual Life to the Fullest.* Charlotte, NC: Tan Books, 1991.

Cohen, Leonard. *Book of Mercy.* Toronto, ON: McClelland & Stewart, 1984.

——. *Book of Longing.* Toronto, ON: McClelland & Stewart, 2007.

Dalai Lama. *The Art of Living.* New York: HarperOne, 2009.

Dalai Lama and Victor Chan. *Wisdom of Forgiveness: Intimate Conversations and Journeys.* New York: Riverhead Books, 2004.

Day, Dorothy. *The Long Loneliness.* New York: Harper & Row, 1952.

——. *The Duty of Delight: The Diaries of Dorothy Day.* Milwaukee: Marquette University Press, 2008.

De Chardin, Teilhard. *Building the Earth.* Wilkes-Barre, PA: Dimension Books, 1965.

——. *Hymn of the Universe.* New York: Harper & Row, 1965.

——. *The Heart of the Matter.* New York: Harcourt, Inc, 2002.

——. *Divine Milieu.* New York: Harper Perennial Modern Classics, 2008.

Forest, Jim. *All Is Grace: A Biography of Dorothy Day.* Maryknoll, NY: Orbis, 2011.

Firestone, Rabbi Tirzah. *Wounds into Wisdom: Healing Generational Jewish Trauma.* Rhinebeck, NY: Monkfish, 2022.

Frey, Karianna, MS, ed. *We Are Beloved: 30 Days with Thea Bowman* (Great Spiritual Teachers). Notre Dame, IN: Ave Maria Press, 2021.

Gaines, Ernest J. *A Lesson Before Dying.* New York: Knopf, 1993.

Galeano, Eduardo. *Genesis: Memory of Fire* (Volume 1); *Faces and Masks* (Volume 2); *Century of Wind* (Volume 3). New York: Nation Books, 2009.

——. *Mirrors: Stories of Almost Everyone.* New York: Nation Books, 2009.

——. *Children of the Days.* New York: Nation Books, 2013.

Gorman, Amanda. *Call Us What We Carry: Poems.* New York: Viking Books, 2021.

——. *The Hill We Climb: An Inaugural Poem for the Country.* New York: Viking Books, 2021.

——. *There Is Always Light: A Journal.* New York: Viking Books, 2022.

Harjo, Joy. *How We Became Human: New and Selected Poems 1975–2001.* New York: W.W. Norton & Company, 2002.

——. *Conflict Resolution for Holy Beings.* New York: W.W. Norton & Company, 2015.

——. *An American Sunrise.* New York: W.W. Norton & Company, 2019.

——. *Poet Warrior: A Memoir.* New York: W.W. Norton & Company, 2021.

——. *Weaving Sundown in a Scarlet Light: 50 Poems for 50 Years.* New York: W.W. Norton & Company, 2022.

——. *Remember.* New York: Random House Studio, 2023.

Herda, D.J. *Wilma Mankiller: How One Woman United the Cherokee Nation and Helped Change the Face of America.* Guilford, CT: TwoDot, 2021.

Heschel, Abraham Joshua. *A Passion for Truth.* Middletown, CT: Wesleyan University Press, 1973.

——. *Moral Grandeur and Spiritual Audacity.* New York: Farrar, Straus and Giroux, 1996.

——. *The Prophets.* New York: HarperCollins, 2001.

——. *The Sabbath.* New York: Farrar, Straus and Giroux, 2005.

——. *Essential Writings.* Maryknoll, NY: Orbis Books, 2011.

——. *I Asked for Wonder: A Spiritual Anthology.* New York: Crossroad, 2020.

Hogan, Linda. *Dwellings: A Spiritual History of the Living World.* New York: W.W. Norton & Company, 2007.

hooks, bell. *All about Love: New Visions* (Love Song to the Nation, 1). New York: William Morrow and Company, 2000.

——. *Salvation: Black People and Love* (Love Song to the Nation, 2). New York: William Morrow and Company, 2001.

——. *Communion: The Female Search for Love* (Love Song to the Nation, 3). New York: William Morrow and Company, 2002.

——. *Ain't I a Woman: Black Women and Feminism.* New York: Routledge, 2015.

——. *Forgive Everyone Everything.* Chicago: Loyola Press, 2022.

——. *Yearning: Race, Gender, and Cultural Politics.* Boston: South End Press, 1999.

Hosseini, Khaled. *The Kite Runner.* New York: Riverhead Books, 2003.

Hurston, Zora Neale. *Their Eyes Were Watching God.* New York: Harper Perennial Modern Classics, 2006.

——. *Every Tongue Got to Confess.* New York: Harper Perennial Modern Classics, 2020.

Jackson, Joe. *Black Elk: The Life of an American Visionary.* New York: Ferrar, Straus and Giroux, 2016.

Kimmerer, Robin Wall. *Gathering Moss: A Natural and Cultural History of Mosses.* Corvallis, OR: Oregon State University Press, 2003.

——. *Braiding Sweetgrass: Indigenous Wisdom, Scientific Knowledge and the Teachings of Plants.* Minneapolis: Milkweed Editions, 2013.

Kingsolver, Barbara. *The Poisonwood Bible.* New York: HarperFlamingo, 1999.

——. *Small Wonder: Essays.* New York: HarperCollins, 2002.

——. *Flight Behavior.* New York: Harper, 2012.

——. *Unsheltered.* New York: Harper, 2018.

King Jr., Martin Luther. *Strength to Love.* Minneapolis: Fortress Press, 2010.

——. *Letter from a Birmingham Jail.* New York: HarperOne, 2015.

——. *I Have a Dream: 60th Anniversary Edition.* New York: HarperOne, 2023.

Kushner, Harold S. *The Lord Is My Shepherd: Healing Wis-*

dom of the 23rd Psalm. New York: Knopf, 2003.

——. *When Bad Things Happen to Good People*. New York: Avon, 2004.

——. *Conquering Fear*. New York: Anchor Books, 2009.

Lee, Pali Jae, and Koko Willis. *Tales from the Night Rainbow*. Honolulu, HI: Night Rainbow Publishing, 1990.

Levine, Amy-Jill. *Sermon on the Mount: A Beginner's Guide to the Kingdom of Heaven*. Nashville: Abingdon Press, 2022.

——. *Signs and Wonders: A Beginner's Guide to the Miracles of Jesus*. Nashville: Abingdon Press, 2022.

——. *The Difficult Words of Jesus: A Beginner's Guide to His Most Perplexing Teachings*. Nashville: Abingdon Press, 2023.

Lewis, C.S. *The Weight of Glory*. New York: HarperOne, 2001.

——. *Mere Christianity*. New York: HarperOne, 2015.

——. *The Problem of Pain*. New York: HarperOne, 2015.

Lewis, John. *Across That Bridge: A Vision for Change and the Future of America*. New York: Hachette Books, 2017.

——. *Good Trouble*. New York: Pushkin Press, 2021.

Lohfink, Gerhard. *The Our Father: A New Reading*. Collegeville, MN: Liturgical Press, 2012.

Lopez, Barry. *Of Wolves and Men*. New York: Scribner, 1978.

——. *Crow and Weasel*. San Francisco: North Point Press, 1990.

——. *Embrace Fearlessly the Burning World: Essays*. New York: Random House, 2023.

Mandela, Ndaba. *Going to the Mountain: Life Lessons from my Grandfather, Nelson Mandela*. New York: Hachette, 2018.

Mandela, Nelson. *Long Walk to Freedom.* Boston: Little, Brown and Company, 1994.

——. *I Know This to Be True.* San Francisco: Chronicle, 2020.

Mankiller, Wilma, Joy Harjo, and Mark N. Trahant. *Mankiller Poems: The Lost Poetry of the Principal Chief of the Cherokee Nation.* Seattle, WA: Pulley Press, 2022.

Mankiller, Wilma, Louise Erdrich, Vine Deloria, and Gloria Steinem. *Every Day Is a Good Day: Reflections by Contemporary Indigenous Women.* Golden, CO: Fulcrum Publishing, 2011.

McCaslin, Wanda D., ed. "Healing as Justice: The Navajo Response to Crime," in *Justice as Healing: Indigenous Ways.* St Paul, MN: Living Justice Press, 2005.

McGrath, Michael O'Neill. *This Little Light: Lessons in Living from Sister Thea Bowman.* Maryknoll, NY: Orbis Books, 2014.

Merton, Thomas. *Seeds of Contemplation.* Norfolk, CT: New Directions, 1949.

——. *The Sign of Jonas.* New York: Harcourt Brace, 1953.

——. *No Man Is an Island.* New York: Harcourt Brace, 1955.

——. *New Seeds of Contemplation.* New York: New Directions, 1961.

——. *Seeds of Destruction.* New York: Farrar, Straus and Giroux, 1964.

——. *Conjectures of a Guilty Bystander.* Garden City, NY: Doubleday, 1966.

——. *Rain and the Rhinoceros.* New York: New Directions, 1973.

——. *Thomas Merton: Essential Writings.* Maryknoll, NY: Orbis Books, 2000.
——. *Love and Living.* New York: HarperOne, 2002.
Metzger, Deena. *Writing for Your Life: Discovering the Story of Your Life's Journey.* New York: HarperOne, 1992.
Morrison, Toni. *Sula.* New York: Knopf, 1973.
——. *Beloved.* New York: Knopf, 1987.
——. *A Mercy.* New York: Knopf, 2008.
——. *God Help the Child.* New York: Knopf, 2015.
Myers, Walter Dean. *I've Seen the Promised Land: The Life of Dr. Martin Luther King, Jr.* New York: HarperCollins, 2004.
Neihardt, John G. *Black Elk Speaks: The Complete Edition.* Lincoln, NE: Bison Books, 2014.
Nikondeha, Kelley, *The First Advent in Palestine: Reversals, Resistance, and the Ongoing Complexity of Hope.* Minneapolis: Broadleaf Books, 2022.
Nutt, Maurice J., CSsR. *Thea Bowman: Faithful and Free* (People of God). Collegeville, MN: Liturgical, 2019.
Ortiz, Dianna. *The Blindfold's Eyes: My Journey from Torture to Truth.* Maryknoll, NY: Orbis Books, 2002.
Pérennès, Jean-Jacques. *A Life Poured Out: Pierre Claverie of Algeria.* Maryknoll, NY: Orbis Books, 2007.
Prejean, Helen. *Dead Man Walking.* New York: Vintage Books, 1994.
——. *River of Fire: My Spiritual Journey.* New York: Random House, 2019.
Proctor, Edna Dean. *Life Thoughts Gathered from the Extem-*

poraneous Discourses of Henry Ward Beecher. Edinburgh: Alexander Strahan, 1858.

Remen, Rachel Naomi. *My Grandfather's Blessings*. New York: Riverhead Books, 2000.

——. *Kitchen Table Wisdom*. New York: Riverhead Books, 2006.

Rittner, Carol, and Sondra Myers. *Courage to Care–Rescuers of Jews during the Holocaust*. New York: NYU Press, 1986.

Romero, Oscar. *Voice of the Voiceless*. Maryknoll, NY: Orbis Books, 1985.

——. *The Violence of Love*. Maryknoll, NY: Orbis Books, 2003.

——. *The Scandal of Redemption*. Walden, NY: Plough Publishing House, 2018.

Roy, Arundhati. *The Cost of Living*. New York: Modern Library, 1999.

——. *The God of Small Things*. New York: Random House, 1997.

——. *Walking with the Comrades*. New York: Penguin, 2011.

——. *The End of Imagination*. Chicago: Haymarket Books, 2016.

Soelle, Dorothee. *Suffering*. Philadelphia, PA: Fortress Press, 1975.

——. *The Window of Vulnerability: A Political Spirituality*. Minneapolis: Fortress Press, 1990.

——. *The Silent Cry: Mysticism and Resistance*. Minneapolis: Fortress Press, 2001.

——. *Essential Writings*. Maryknoll, NY: Orbis Books, 2005.

——. *Death by Bread Alone.* Maryknoll, NY: Orbis Books, 2008.

Solnit, Rebecca. *A Field Guide to Getting Lost.* New York: Penguin, 2005.

——. *Men Explain Things to Me.* Chicago: Haymarket Books, 2014.

——. *Evening Thoughts.* Chicago: Haymarket Books, 2016.

——. *Hope in the Dark: Untold Histories, Wild Possibilities.* Chicago: Haymarket Books, 2016.

——. *The Mother of All Questions.* Chicago: Haymarket Books, 2017.

Sorell, Traci, and Chelsea Clinton. *She Persisted: Wilma Mankiller.* New York: Philomel, 2022.

West, Cornel. *Race Matters.* Boston: Beacon Press, 2001.

——. *Democracy Matters.* New York: Penguin, 2005.

Wiesel, Elie. *Five Biblical Portraits.* Notre Dame, IN: University of Notre Dame Press, 1981.

——. *Night Trilogy: Night, Dawn, Day.* New York: Hill and Wang, 2008.

Williams, Terry Tempest. *Finding Beauty in a Broken World.* New York: Vintage, 2009.

——. *When Women Were Birds: Fifty-four Variations on Voice.* New York: Picador, 2013.

——. *Erosion: Essays of Undoing.* New York: Sarah Crichton Books, 2019.

——. "Unraveling," *Emergence Magazine.* May 12, 2022.

Wolfelt, Alan. *365 Days of Understanding Your Grief.* Fort Collins, CO: Companion Press, 2021.